The Banana Empire
New Orleans International Power

by

Richard Edgar Zwez

Published by Write2Grow LLC
ISBN: 978-1-79484-693-7

W2G Publishing
Write2Grow LLC
Luling, Louisiana

www.write2grow.org

DEDICATION

To all the sweet people who have been in my life.

Table of Contents

Chapter One
The New Conquistadors

Who are these people? Do they think they're better than us? It's a question that is asked with increasing frequency and with greater vigor as centuries pass and erode past achievements of empire builders such as the conquistadors in the eyes of the native people. The empire slips away. What's more slippery than one built on bananas?

Novelty and innovations such as guns brought by the invaders become commonplace and admiration towards the strangers who built the empire diminishes.

But that comes later. The zeal of the creator of the empire initially burns like a bright flame. At first, it's a beacon that mesmerizes the faces it illuminates. The United Fruit Company was a multinational company, also known as "La Frutera," with banana fruit-growing business interests in Central America, South America, and the Caribbean. It had profitability as its main interest. To reach this objective, it employed many tactics of a ruthless nature just as a corrupting governments.

It did whatever it took to build and sustain a commercial empire. As an enterprise, its appearance was markedly American and at times did not hesitate to call upon the United States to use its power.

Its use of chemicals to control plant disease was such that they contributed to environmental damage. It also ruined the environment by running drainage canals that led to erosion and to the pollution of waterways, estuaries, and coral reefs as the banana waste such as the discarded banana stalks and stems as well as bananas that were unsightly were dumped into streams and rivers leading to damage and death to organisms through oxygen depletion as they decomposed.

The Company's might was such that it controlled in a given country as much as eighty percent of the land available for cultivation. This included land that it wasn't using but held in reserve. This was true in the case of farms struck by banana blight. As the land became infected so that the bananas died, it would abandon the plantation and start a new one on land not previously planted.

It also prevented local farmers from participating in the banana business. It left thousands of acres of land idle while the native population had to scrounge for any piece of land to cultivate including hills. The hardscrabble life that resulted for the peasants led to their constant poverty.

To build an empire, you have to mold it with whatever procedures are needed. Knowing how to handle what's on hand makes all the difference between success and failure. To this end, while exploiting the land of the host nation as it pleased, the Company reduced to a minimum the contribution it could possibly give to the countries whose land it exploited. It tried to keep the taxes paid to the government of the host nation reduced to little if anything.

And it held down the wages of its workers. For their hard work they never were able to gain much for their sweat. They always earned less than ten percent of the bananas' retail value sometimes only one to three percent. Even child laborers as young as eight toiled in the banana plantations. They could work as much as twelve hours a day, seven days a week.

And the workers were never protected from the agricultural chemicals. Huge quantities of fungicides, pesticides, herbicides, fertilizers, and chemically impregnated plastic stem coverings were used in the desire of growing perfect bananas. The health of the workers consequently suffered considerably through diseases and conditions such as cancers and immune-destroying diseases as well as impotence and sterility in men and the list continues on. And even their women were affected with numerous stillbirths and miscarriages.

The same problems occurred in the plantations of Honduras, Guatemala, Nicaragua, Costa Rica, Panama, Colombia, Ecuador, Cuba, Jamaica, and the Dominican Republic.

The question remains of how sincere are both United Fruit, now known as Chiquita Brands, and Standard Fruit, now called Dole, in correcting the health damaging procedures inflicted on their laborers.

Dole used a preparation called Nemagon as a nematicide. It killed the tiny worms that would feed on the roots of the banana plants. But it produced awful effects on humans as have been mentioned. These evils were known as early as the 1950s, but it kept on using Nemagon into the 1990s.

United Fruit also found other ways to make money. It collected tariffs in and out on products of the countries it serviced through its fleet of steamships called The Great White Fleet with its distinctive diamond painted on the smokestacks. It increased its profits by having cabins for tourists while carrying bananas in its ships' holds. It also discouraged the building of highways in countries where it had its interest so that travelers would pay fares on its company-owned railroads.

What would happen if people opposed the ruthless exploitation of United Fruit by going on strike? It would then leave the area after destroying its housing, including the buildings providing needed services such as schools, and would even tear up the railroads. The offending area would be left with its sustenance greatly impaired.

Unfortunately, situations are bound to change and then what? How long will an empire last? Empires are often built over native people and while doing so disguise their names. For example, the United Fruit Company in Honduras went under the name of Tela Railroad Company.

The English Language was preferred for all of its management and in its top dealings. Managers were United States citizens and others who were not Americans but who spoke English.

In the cities where it had business interests, it built sections exclusive to its employees. In the case of Tela, Honduras, there was Tela Vieja where native

Hondurans resided, and then separated by a river there was Tela Nueva where the company had its people living considerably well in new, improved housing.

Resentment built up, particularly if the natives of a country were considered inferior in many ways. They lived in barracks-like housing while the white managing elite enjoyed much better single-family homes.

There's a Spanish saying that an evil never lasts a hundred years since who could put up with it that long? With the passing of time, the native people become increasingly aware of being mistreated.

As the legacy of the Spanish in the conquest of the Americas by the Conquistadores became transformed into new rich Hispanic cultures, a new conquering entity rose up just as the last remains of the Spanish

Empire were finished off by the United States in the Spanish American War.

In 1899 the United Fruit Company appeared and received concessions from the favorable governments where it cultivated bananas. It always had in mind its interests

and not those of the host countries. For example, it promised to build railroads in exchange for land concessions. It did. But those railroads were constructed to allow the bananas to be exported from the ports it dominated and not in the interests of the country that had been generous to it. Honduras, the country most identified as being a banana republic, was left as the only country in Central America whose capitol city, Tegucigalpa, was not reachable by rail.

With such a powerful reach the United Fruit Company whose tentacles of power grasped everywhere while seeking to further its interests by whatever ruthless means necessary, received from its enemies the name “el pulpo”: “the octopus.”

In New Orleans, noted for its distinctive and varied architectural styles, you may not give a second glance to a sculptural doorway situated on 321 St. Charles Avenue. It’s a busy thoroughfare with rushing streetcars and considerable traffic, and anyone’s gaze may be attracted somewhere else by the bustling activity, outstanding buildings, and enticing festivities. For example, nearby exists the enormous World War II Museum that’s constantly undergoing improvements.

The doorway has raised lettering telling you that’s it’s the entrance to the United Fruit Company headquarters. No person’s name is glorified by being mentioned on its façade. The year 1920 does appear sculpted on it.

Anyone knowing the history of the United Fruit Company might have expect the name of Sam Zemurray included in the inscription of this doorway. But Sam Zemurray, AKA as “Sam the Banana Man,” the principal owner of the United Fruit Company in that year was not as powerful then as he would become. By 1930 he had absorbed twenty rival banana companies and become the greatest employer in Central America. His superintendents extended and consolidated the Company’s grip by controlling the lives of its workers in every area of life.

Whoever came up with the figure of the Company as an outreaching octopus, struck up a colossal monster taking over country after country in Hispanic America.

This menacing creature's long arms covered with suckers went on to position themselves on every area of existence. The big saucer eyes searched to grasp additional lucrative possibilities. The huge head tried to decide what should be its next move. And its ink—to be used to legally document and support any of its actions. But the ink also employed power to smear the visions of its maneuvers in order to hide its true intentions as it sought to manipulate reality to its own designs. What about its parrot beak? It was effective to cut down any competitors in tropical areas. Or any troublesome ideas such as nationalism.

Did people develop a taste for octopus? Many did. The power of the United Fruit Company provided benefits to those willing to go along with its business operations.

Despite its misdeeds the Company provided for its workers fine medical care, rent-free housing in its barracks style buildings, and six years of tuition-free schooling. Other than the environmental damage, the Company brought under cultivation land that was unproductive such as that was obtained through the drainage of swamps.

To really get a clear understanding of this banana empire and how it affected the everyday lives of those living under it, you must have experienced the effects of its operations. The Tela Railroad Company created a way of life that now no longer exists since it conducted its business as an entity with its own world that influenced every aspect of those persons' lives.

While the United Fruit Company out of Tela exploited the land in Honduras, its main headquarters was in the town of Bananera located in Guatemala. The other banana company, the Standard Fruit Company, was also ruthless. It had been founded by the Vaccaro Brothers from New Orleans and operated out of the city of La Ceiba in Honduras. When the land records in the city hall burned, it was able to reshuffle the territory to its own advantage.

Company life had many interesting features that were positive and delightful especially to those who were privileged within the organization.

At times, there were exciting adventures in Honduras whose North Coast was, despite man's encroachment, still under the influence of the wild, surrounding tropical rain forest and the rest of nature's other dominant powers including its powerful weather systems. There were also fine people to be acquainted with while operating under the dominance of the Company as well as others whose passions could pose a threat.

All in all, life in the Company world was so uniquely admirable in its positive aspects that you will never see its likes again. It's a lost world that disappeared after it surrendered the manner in which it operated its empire.

References

Karnes, Thomas L. *Tropical Enterprise: The Standard Fruit & Steamship Company in Latin America.* Baton Rouge: Louisiana State University Press, 1978.

Kepner, Charles David and Jay Soothill. *The Banana Empire: A Case Study of Economic Imperialism.* New York: Russell & Russell, 1967.

Martin, Chris. "Bananas—The Facts." *Internationalist,* October 5, 1999.

Mccan, Thomas. *An American Company: The Tragedy of United Fruit.* New York: Crown, 1976.

Moore, Kailyn. "The True History of Dole, Banana Plantations, Chemical Pesticides and Human Suffering." *Tags*, June 23, 2011.

Moskan, Tura. "Helping the Third World One Banana at a Time." *New York Times,* May 5, 2004.

Vargas, Gerardo. *The Socio-Environmental Problems of Banana Plantations in Costa Rica.* Costa Rica: Foro Emaus, 1998.

Wilson, Charles. *Empire in Green and Gold: The Story of the American Banana Trade.* New York: Holt, 1947.

Chapter Two
Desire for Dominance

The national hymn of Honduras poetically expresses in its first stanza that the country was like a beautiful virgin Indian maiden who was awakened from her sleep by the intrepid navigator, meaning no doubt Columbus. He named the country Honduras meaning "depths" because of the profound water along the coast. In fact, he dropped anchors and found out that the couldn't reach the bottom of the sea.

The Spanish followed discovery of the new lands with conquest and exploitation. By then the native Americans would be shaken awake by the selfish intentions of the conquistadors.

The citizens of the United States who arrived in Honduras to head the United Fruit Company and its subsidiary, Tela Railroad Company, were not the first to arrive in Honduras fired with the conquering spirit.

The cacique, word in Spanish for Indian chief, called Cucumba, found himself dispossessed by the Spanish who took over for themselves a location that provided clean water and food as well as a splendid bay. Tetela in the Nahua language referred to the hills around the town. The Spanish shortened it to Tela after they founded their colony on the 3rd of May, 1524. The founder of the colony was Cristóbal de Olid sent by the Hernán Cortés the conqueror of Mexico. However, Olid decided he wanted the colony all to himself. So, Cortés had to send his cousin to overthrow the insurrection. This led to a chain of numerous other conflicts among the Spanish. Finally, Cortés himself had to come down from Mexico to stop the infighting. In addition, the conquistadors had to deal with native uprisings.

To make matters even worse, English privateers and pirates prowled the waters around the colony. One of their favorite activities was to go around the Caribbean and burn down Spanish settlements.

Honduras became independent on September 15, 1821, along with the other Central American countries. Thereafter there were attempts to form all of the Central American nations into a confederation but the countries decided to go their own separate ways.

Honduras until 1932 was convulsed by civil wars, the so-called "revolutions." To complicate matters further the United States kept intervening into Hispanic American countries after 1898 when it defeated Spain in the Spanish American War. For example, United States troops got involved in both Honduras and the Dominican Republic politics in 1903. In 1907 they're back in Honduras and Nicaragua. And returned to Nicaragua in 1909. In 1912 the U.S. intervened in Cuba, Panama, and Honduras. And so forth for decades. Peace came to the region at a high price when ruthless dictators took over with Ubico in Guatemala, Hernández in San Salvador, Somoza in Nicaragua, and Carías in Honduras. These dictators brought about the political and social stability so much desired by the banana companies to carry out their business enterprises. But there remained the constant worry of communist penetration in Hispanic countries as the United States and the Soviet Union competed for world dominance.

The desire for total control in Honduras by the United Fruit Company and in Tela, Honduras, its base of operations was typical of the events that took place throughout the banana empire. The Americans, like the white men from Spain who first arrived in Tela were fueled by the twin goals of being dominant and domineering.

References:

Díaz, Bernal. *The Conquest of New Spain.* Translated by J. M. Cohen. New York: Penguin Books, 1963.

Dodd, Thomas J. *Tiburcio Carías: Portrait of a Honduran Political Leader.* Baton Rouge: Louisiana State University Press, 2005.

Dosal, Paul J. *Doing Business with Dictators: A Political History of United Fruit in Guatemala, 1899*-1944. Wilmington, DE: SR Books, 1993.

Krehn, William. *Democracies and Tyrannies of the Caribbean in the 1940s.* Toronto: Lugus Libros, 1999.

Luque, Gonzalo R. *Memorias de un sampedrano (Memoires of a San Pedro Sula Citizen)* San Pedro Sula: Impresora Hondureña,1979.

_____. *Memorias de un soldado Hondureño (Memoires of a Honduran Soldier)* San Pedro Sula: Impresora Hondureña, 1980.

_____. *Las revoluciones de Honduras (The Revolutions of Honduras)* San Pedro Sula, Impresora Hondureña, 1982.

Stone, Samuel Z. *The Heritage of the Conquistadors : Ruling Classes of Central America from the Conquest to the Sandinistas*. Lincoln: University of Nebraska Press, 1990.

Chapter Three
Banana Struggles

To add to the political turbulence of constant revolutions that existed in the Hispanic countries there arose conflicts among the competitors for the dominance of the banana markets.

Bananas were largely unknown to American consumers. It wasn't until a Captain Lorenzo Dow Baker bought 160 bunches of bananas in Jamaica in 1870 for the low price of a shilling per bunch and found out that in Jersey City he could sell the bananas for two dollars apiece. Baker was encouraged by his success. So, he and Andrew Preston of Boston decided to develop a banana market in Boston and created the Boston Fruit Company. They chose Preston to take charge of the tropical banana management while Baker would manage the company from Boston.

In the meantime, another fellow, Minor Copper Keith, helped his uncle, Henry Meiggs, complete a railroad in Costa Rica. Keith used bananas to cheaply feed his railroad workers. When the railroad was completed, he used it to export bananas from plantations he had planted in the 1870s. He had entered a successful business. To add to it he decided to buy a controlling fifty percent stock in the Snyder Banana Company that produced bananas in Panama in 1897. Keith also established a bank, but it went bankrupt and lost money. So he went to Boston and arranged to merge his company with Preston's. Baker and Keith went on to establish the United Fruit Company in 1899.

The new company then became larger after it bought out also in 1899 seven companies that were in Honduras. In 1903, United Fruit bought a fifty percent of the stock owned by the Elders and Fyffes Company who had been exporting bananas to Europe, and so it also entered into that market.

This same year United Fruit purchased the S.S. Venus as its first refrigerated ship. But the Company had the misfortune to have its banana trees attacked by the Panama Disease that struck the roots and cut off the water supply. In 1901, the government of Guatemala asked United Fruit to operate its mail service. And in 1904 it granted to it a concession for ninety-nine years to run the railroad between Guatemala City and the main port of Puerto Barrios.

In 1912, United Fruit additionally took over the Atlantic Fruit Company in Costa Rica when this competitor declared bankruptcy. It now controlled the banana export business emanating from that country. In 1913, the Honduran government granted to United Fruit two railroad concessions and were managed by two subsidiaries, the Tela Railroad Company and the Trujillo Railroad Company. Thus, United Fruit could grow bananas on a massive scale on 162,000 acres of which 71,000 had been granted through railroad construction. United Fruit got a big break when it got the United States government to allow the importation of bananas tax free. In 1924, United Fruit gained a concession from the Guatemalan government on uncultivated land on an area of one hundred kilometers. But in 1927 the Guatemalan government asked for $14,000 rent on this same territory. United Fruit further expanded its business by purchasing the California-Guatemala Fruit Corporation whose business was to export bananas to Western United States from the Guatemalan Pacific Coast.

A man appeared on the banana commerce scene who would have a huge impact on the United Fruit Company and the overall banana business. He was born Schmuel Zmurri in January 18, 1877, at the time of the Russian Empire in Kishinev, Bessarabia, now known as Chisinau in Moldova in a poor Jewish family. His family immigrated to the United States in 1892 and initially settled in Selma, Alabama. With his named changed to Samuel Zemurray in 1895, he began a local banana business at the age of eighteen by selling fruit that had ripened too soon aboard ship and would have been discarded by United Fruit in Mobile, Alabama. He sold to peddlers and grocers along the railroad line.

By 1900 Zemurray had been successful enough to join forces with another investor, Ashbell Hubbard. They acquired two tramp steamers to carry the bananas bought from independent growers and then sell them in Mobile and New Orleans. In 1910 the two entrepreneurs then went on to purchase five thousand acres along the Cuyamel River in Honduras to create their own banana exporting business. They shipped their fruit out of a tiny port called Omoa.

But they discovered that President Miguel Dávila would not grant them land, transportation, and tax concessions that they were seeking. So Zemurray organized and financed a military coup headed by Guy

"Machine Guy" Molony to install a former president of Honduras, Manuel Bonilla, as the new president. Once installed he granted Zemurray the concession to a large tract of land he desired and also allowed him to incorporate his Hubbard-Zemurray company and to operate tax free for the next twenty-five years. This same year Zemurray bought the remaining stock of Elders and Fyffes that owned eight thousand acres for banana production in the Canary Islands. Then in 1911 Hubbard-Zemuray company changed its name to the Cuyamel Fruit Company.

By 1922 it had bought out the Bluefields Fruit and Steamship Company. And the number of ships it owned had grown to thirteen including the purchase of some of them from surplus United States ships used during the First World War. The shipping came out of ports of Honduras and Nicaragua headed to New Orleans. But United Fruit found out that it would not be the only substantial enterprise dealing with bananas. It had a serious competitor.

Once again, the importance of New Orleans in the banana business was highlighted when immigrants this time from Sicily, the Vaccaro brothers, Joseph, Luca, and Felix, together with Salvador D'Antoni began importing the fruit from La Ceiba, Honduras, to New Orleans.

Their success was so great that by 1915 they had a tremendous need for ice to refrigerate their ships. Joseph, as president of the Vaccaro Brothers Company, had to start buying most of the ice manufactured in New Orleans. So much so that he became known as the "Ice King."

After the outbreak of the First World War, the United States wanted to declare a complete embargo on the importation of bananas, so the ships of the United Fruit Company and the Vaccaro Brothers Company were to be incorporated into the war effort. But fortunately for the two companies the idea was dismissed. In 1924, it was time for a name change. This company became known as the Standard Fruit Company, and in 1926 the name changed once more to the Standard Fruit and Steamship Company. This company just like United Fruit that had engaged in the political and economic subversion of the governments Central American countries to gain the best favorable business situations for its activities, did the same in Honduras.

To the dismay of the banana companies, the Panama Disease had begun attacking their banana trees not only in that country but also in Guatemala, Nicaragua, and Costa Rica. It is a plant disease, a fungal pathogen, that attacks the roots of the banana tree and cannot be controlled with chemicals. It managed to destroy the Gros Michel banana type that was the principal variety. The Cavendish type of banana took its place.

Zemurray had an uncanny ability to view with accurate assessment banana production possibilities. United Fruit had been growing its bananas in Costa Rica, Guatemala, and Jamaica. Zemurray proved that in Honduras, by his knowledge of banana cultivation, he could bring into production land that seemingly was unsuitable for growing bananas. It was indeed a country where bananas could be grown very profitably.

After being in a prize war that pitted United Fruit against the Cuyamel Fruit Company. United Fruit bought out Zemurray in 1930 for $31,500,000 and thus made him its largest shareholder. with 300,000 shares.

In 1930 Huey Long of Louisiana denounced United Fruit for conducting corrupt business practices in Central America. In Guatemala, Juan Pablo Wainwright led a banana strike against United Fruit. The movement was crushed, and he was in turn assassinated.

When Zemurray obtained his large fortune in stock he decided to retire. But, alas, not for long. The United Fruit company stock started to plummet. It went from $158 a share in 1929 to $10 in 1932. It was time for "Sam, the Banana Man" to take over as managing director in charge of operations. He held this position until 1938. He decided that a vigorous man needed to be at the helm of the Company. It had to be led by being out in the field and not by being directed from Boston. While in power he fired and replaced many employees especially those who were slow to act and to decide what needed to be done. He often placed in charge managers who had worked for him when he owned the Cuyamel Fruit Company. Superfluous employees were removed with as many as twenty-five percent discharged.

He found out that the banana boats were leaving port half-full. He made sure that from then on they left fully loaded. He sold excess ships, mothballed some, or rented out space in them.

He became the world's largest banana grower and added to the Company's the cultivation of cacao and other products of tropical products such as sugar cane and African oil palms.

What the Company needed was political stability in Central America. The countries had dreadful histories of national governments constantly being overthrown by revolutions within the country or by the bringing of armed insurgents into the nation from a neighboring nation.

The solution was to install dictators who would provide the necessary peaceful continuation of power that would in turn stabilize the business arrangements that the banana fruit company needed to carry on its successes.

In 1934 dictator Anastasio Somaza of Nicaragua, who favored United Fruit, became president. His family would run the country into the 1970s. In 1936, Guatemalan dictator Jorge Ubico gave United Fruit a ninety-nine-year concession so that it could open a second plantation. In addition, the dictator of San Salvador, Hernández Martínez, and that of Honduras, Carías, with their repressive regimes provided the United Fruit with the stability to conduct its banana business in Central America during the 1930s and 1940s.

In 1937, United Fruit expanded to incorporate Minor Keith's International Railways of Central America.

In the early 1930s the Sigatoka disease appeared. It is a fungus that attacks the leaves of the bananas and causes the fruit to mature prematurely. It first appeared in the Standard Fruit's Honduran plantations. The bananas have to be sprayed by using the Bourdeaux mixture that consists of copper sulfate, hydrated lime, and water. It works but is very expensive.

To back up his increasingly expensive operations Zemurray had the Great White Fleet to carry out his transportation needs. The Fleet transported bananas but also other freight, mail, and passengers in increasing numbers by energizing tourism on its ships that sported available cabins and entertaining activities such as parties and delicious food throughout the Caribbean, Central and South America, Europe, and Africa. By 1940 the Fleet sailed sixty-one ships with an additional eleven chartered. Zemurray could also count with additional twenty-three vessels from a British affiliate. So, the Great White Fleet became the largest privately-owned fleet in private hands.

During World War Two, the United Fruit Company shipping went to war. The twenty-three ships that were British flagged were impressed into the British Navy and mostly served as troop carriers. The United States War Department followed that example and took over most of the Great White Fleet, leaving Zemurray with the clunkers. Then he lost some to German submarines. As the ships went down, so went the profits. The Company also lost twenty percent of its market during the war when the British declared that bananas were a luxury and ceased their importation to England and its colonies. And the United States War slapped bananas with a quota.

Zemurray found other products that were necessary for the war effort and did not have a quota with the growing of hemp, quinine, and rubber plants.

In 1945, Guatemalan President Arevalo forced United Fruit to reform its working conditions.

In 1947, with the Guatemalan government enforced a Labor Code. United Fruit denounced it as being communistic and threatened to leave the country.

In Honduras, 1949, with the departure of former dictator, Carías, the newly elected government of Juan Manuel Gálvez passed legislation for the protection of child labor and establishment of the eight-hour day. Now the Company was beginning to feel the pinch of having to adhere to government regulations of the host countries where up to now it had free reign to impose its will without having to worry about restrictions.

Zemurray retired in 1951 but remained as chairman of the executive committee of the Company with continuing interest in Central American politics.

When Jacobo Arbenz became president of Guatemala in 1951 he pushed through the Guatemalan Congress in 1952 an Agrarian Reform Act that required United Fruit to give up uncultivated land and would compensate the Company with government bonds. Zemurray responded by negatively portraying Arbenz as a communist in the American media and published a book, "Report on Guatemala," that claimed that the Guatemalan Agrarian Reform Act was developed in the Soviet Union, and he distributed the book to the American Congress.

In 1954, American Secretary of State John Foster Dulles protested that the amount to be paid to United Fruit was unfair. In June of this same year Guatemala was invaded from Honduras by Carlos Castillo Armas. The Eisenhower administration helped him with the support of the CIA. Arbenz was overthrown, and United Fruit got its lands back.

Castillo Armas went on to identify 70,000 citizens, or about 10 % of the Guatemalan population, as having communistic leanings and subject to severe punishment. With him began the Guatemalan Civil War which ended in 1996 after approximately 200,000 deaths.

Then in May of 1954, Honduran workers of United Fruit went on strike for better working conditions and were joined by those of Standard Fruit. In July when the strike ended there was a twenty-one percent raise for the workers and improved labor standards.

But the actions of the United Fruit to hold on to its land holdings by all means necessary came to an end in 1958, when it was forced by anti-trust actions of the United States to give up some of its holdings. This led to United Fruit changing the way it did business. It decided to get out of the growing of bananas area of business. Now individual entrepreneurs would raise the bananas and the Company be in charge of transportation, marketing, and distribution of the fruit. Thus, the Company maintained control while eliminating the hassles of production.

Zemurray despite his many business preoccupations had married Sarah Weinberger in 1904 and had a daughter, and a son who was killed while serving in World War Two in the Army Air Corps. Zemurray died in 1961 from Parkinson's disease in New Orleans. The city had been his home for many years.

The United Fruit Company with its new way of conducting its business changed its name to Chiquita Brands. The Standard Fruit Company became Dole after it was acquired between 1964 and 1968 by the Castle & Cook Corporation that had also included at the same time in its holdings the James Dole Hawaiian Pineapple Company.

But did the change of name of these companies necessarily reformed totally their philosophy of making money above all considerations?

Dole for its part in 2010 was accused of making payments to a paramilitary organization called United Auto-Defense Forces of Colombia (AUC) fighting in Colombia. I had done so to protect its business operations from interference from insurgent groups fighting the government and increasingly operating in the countryside.

Chiquita also made at least one hundred payments to AUC for a total of $1.7 million. It also paid terrorists. It was fined by the U.S. federal government twenty-five million dollars for making security payments to them from 1997 to 2004. Basically, it was a protection racket scheme.

Chiquita continued its attempts to influence the political decisions of the countries that grew its bananas. In 1985 Costa Rica passed its Banana Promotion Plan that made the banana producers happy by making for favorable tax benefits and exchange rates and the desired deregulation of laws pertaining to labor and the environment.

In 1975 Chiquita was caught in what became known as Bananagate when the U.S. Securities and Exchange Commission exposed that the president of Honduras, Oswaldo López Arellano, had been bribed with one and a quarter million dollars and the promise of the same amount later in order to obtain a reduction in export taxes.

In the meantime, the exploitation of the workers on the banana plantations continues. At present, thirty percent of the laborers are permanent. Seventy percent have only ninety-day contracts that forces them to go from plantation to plantation seeking employment. By becoming migrant workers, they lose out from not having social security and many other benefits.

The banana producing countries' economies also suffer. Due to the uneven distribution of land, they are forced to increase their grain imports. In Honduras between 1960 and 1993 the production of grains decreased thirty-one percent.

The corrupt exploitation of Honduras by the multinationals through the cooperation of willing governments was already obvious when the American writer O. Henry (pseudonym of William Sydney Porter), who was living in the country in 1896, fled to Honduras after being wanted for embezzlement in a U.S. bank. O. Henry coined the term "banana republic" when he used it to describe the fictional Republic of Anchuria in his novel *Cabbages and Kings* written in 1904. In it he has a president running off with money from the treasury and intervention by American gunboats.

Latin American writers felt the need to denounce the ruthless exploitation of the countries by the multinationals with their desire to form capitalistic empires. Such was the case by Ramón Amaya Amador of Honduras, Miguel Ángel Asturias and Augusto Monterroso of Guatemala, Carlos Luis Fallas and Carmen Lyra of Costa Rica, and Pablo Neruda of Chile.

An incident that really caught the attention of novelists was a massacre of striking workers of the United Fruit Company. I took place on December 6, 1928 at the town of Ciénaga, Colombia, near the city of Santa Marta. The president of Colombia, Miguel Mendez sent an army regiment from Bogota, the capital of the country. The soldiers set up machine guns on low buildings surrounding the square where the strikers were gathered on this Sunday after Mass. Between 47 and 3,000 people were killed, depending upon which sources are to be believed, whether they be historians and contemporaries for the low number or the survivors and oral histories for the high figure. The killers threw the dead into the sea.

The author Álvaro Cepeda Samudio wrote about the killing in his novel *La Casa Grande*. Nobel literature prize winner of 1967, Gabriel García Marquez, portrayed the massacre in the fictional town of Macondo in his novel masterpiece, *One Hundred Years of Solitude*.

The practices of United Fruit and its successor, Chiquita, have been repeatedly criticized in the United States. In 1950, Gore Vidal in his novel, *Dark Green, Bright Red*, wrote about United Fruit intervening in Guatemala. He felt that the United States had become an imperialist country.

The song "Bitter Fruit" in 1987 by Little Steven reputedly referred to the United Fruit. He tells in his song about working for a company who is far away and not responsive with kindness but is overbearing so now the fruit that once was sweet is bitter. Despite the faults of the Tela Railroad Company in Honduras, as a subsidiary of United Fruit, it can be said with a great deal of truth that it led the country by example through its orderliness, management, sanitation, and law enforcement. The city of Tela has shown a considerable decline in these areas. The beautiful, majestic beach of Tela that while the Company reigned could be strolled in complete safety and ocean lovers did not fear being mugged now is dangerous. Its white sand like fresh tropical snow with its powdery softness invited one to lay on it as if it was a fluffy carpet.

Now it has taken on a yellowish, dirty appearance. The ocean shore has not been kept clear of debris. While the Company supervised life in Tela Nueva, the care it lavished on the beach was such that the coconut palms along it were festively painted white about a yard up their trunks to dress them up. The fact that Zemurray maintained a huge beach house on the splendid beach insured that it would be well taken care of. Zemurray, it was said, only stayed The wonderful Tela wharf suffered both from hurricane and fire and now it's nothing but a pitiful stump. While it stood complete, it was a treat to stand on it and hear the lovely sound of the waves passing underneath. In addition, while using it as a perch it was beautiful to see the moon shining on the ocean while the perfumed sea breeze caressed your body.

The accounting department building in the Tela Nueva section became completely gutted with its concrete walls and with its deserted windows reduced to complete dilapidation and desolation, looking like the eye sockets of an abandoned skull. It has been restored as a Company museum.

Now the Company has shifted its interest to La Lima also in Honduras after the Great Liberating Strike against it centered in Tela defied its power. There is little employment in Tela. A lot of its sorely declined income comes from overseas remittances. The structures that gave Tela Nueva character including the Mess Hall and the hospital have been torn down.

But what of the downtrodden workers at the banana plantations? The whole beneficial structure sponsored by the Company has often collapsed at various plantations with drug trafficking, lack of sanitation, violence, and so forth.

References:

Argueta, Mario. *Bananos y política"Samuel Zemurray y la Cuyamel Fruit Company en Honduras.* Tegucigalpa: Editorial Universitaria, 1987

"Basic Copper Sulfate," *Pesticide Information Profile,* EXTOXNET-Extension Toxicology Network, 5/94-7.

Buchelli, Marcelo, "United Fruit Company in Latin America: Institutional Uncertainties and Changes in its Operations, 1900-1970" *Banana Wars: Power, Production and History in the Americas,* Durham: Duke University Press 2003.

______. *Good Dictator, Bad Dictator: United Fruit Company and Economic Nationalism in Central America,* Urbana: University of Illinois, 2006.

Cohen, Rich. *The Fish That Ate the Whale.* New York: Picador, 2012.

Colby, Jason M. *The Business of Empire: United Fruit, Race, and U.S. Expansion in Central America.* Ithaca: Cornell University Press, 2015.

Coleman, Kevin. "Banana Massacre," *Making the Empire Work and United States Imperialism.* New York: New York University Press 2015.

Dosal. Paul. *Doing Business with Dictators: A Political History of United Fruit in Guatemala 1899-1944,* Wilmington: SR Books, 1993.

Euraque, Darío. *Reinterpreting the Banana Republic: Region and State in Honduras, 1870-1972,* Chapel Hill: University of North Carolina Press. 1996.

"Foreign Relations of the United States, 1952-1954, Volume IV: the American Republics," *United States Department of State.*

Grossman, Lawrence S. *The Political Ecology of Bananas: Contracting Farming, Peasants, and Agrarian Change in the Eastern Caribbean.* Chapel Hill: University of North Carolina Press 1998.

Harrington, Anthony S., Chairman, Intelligence Oversight Board. *Report on the Guatemala Review*, June 28, 1996, 1-4.

"Honduras, General Strike." *Time, May 24, 1954.*

"Peeling Back the Truth on Bananas," *Food Empowerment Project,* 2018, 1-8.

Stephens, Clyde S. *Bananeros in Central America: True Stories of The Tropics,* Alva, Florida: Banana Books, 1989.

Chapter Four
Samuel Zemurray's Dynamics

"Sam, the Banana Man," went from being a very poor immigrant to becoming a multimillionaire entrepreneur. He was often criticized for his ruthless tactics in underdeveloped countries that earned for them the dismal name of "banana republics." On the other hand, he has been praised for having these same countries develop their economies. Zemurray's success can be attributed in large part due to his direct involvement in his business. He got to know the people of the countries where he had his plantations and kept on his on-hands approach to what was happening on the ground. He was an innovator who was adventurous in implementing new approaches to increase banana production. His men cut out inferior fruit stock arising from the ground and in order to have proper drainage he had concrete lined canals to drain off excess water, and he installed extremely tall overhead sprinklers to prevent lack of watering during dry spells.

He appreciated the culture of the countries where he did business. He paid his planation workers for their finds of pre-Columbian Mayan artifacts. These he donated to Tulane University. He also supported archeological efforts of the ancient Mesoamerican Indian sites. I remember reading in the United Fruit Company magazine, Unifruitco, that the Company became involved in the restoration of the ancient Mayan city of Tikal in Guatemala.

He also helped Hispanic American agriculture and disease control with the establishment and support of the Zamorano Pan-American Agricultural school in Honduras. He preferred that the graduates not work for United Fruit but go on their own to develop their individual futures.

But he was interested in helping his employees in the Hispanic American countries to better their lives. This included providing educational opportunities for the common laborers children to attend school on the plantations and also the American schools taught in English to enhance United States culture. The Unifruitco magazine also highlighted the efforts of the Company to make life enjoyable such as building a bowling alley in La Lima, Honduras. He also created outside of Tela, Honduras, the Lancetilla Botanical Gardens that had thousands of species. Some able to promote the production of useful hemp, quinine, and rubber. Back in the United States, he financed left-wing oriented efforts including the magazine, The Nation. He supported the New Deal efforts of President Franklin D. Roosevelt. On the other hand, he attacked the ambitions of Huey P. Long while he dominated Louisiana politics. He had great ambitions including becoming president of the United States.

In New Orleans, the city of his residence, was the recipient of his dynamic philanthropy. He founded the city's hospital to take care of black women and a clinic for crippled and retarded children with his New Orleans Child Guidance Clinic. He was the most prominent financial donor to Tulane University. He created in it the United States' the first center for public health and tropical medicine in a city with a history of yellow fever. He also started the Mayan Art and Middle American Research Institute, which he elevated with the Pre-Columbian cultural finds discovered in his plantations, and now this institution is named for his son-in-law, Roger Thayer Stone. He also forwarded the building of residence halls and a gymnasium at Tulane. He wanted Tulane to be "the Harvard of the South."

And to top off his contribution to this great university, he donated at his death his former residence at 2 Audubon Place as the home of Tulane's president. Its front door faces Audubon Park. It is a magnificent mansion with a multitude of columns not only in its front but also along its sides. It also has a pipe organ, chandelier, and a ball room in its third story. With his usual spirit of innovation, Zemurray, in 1931, placed intercom connections in all of its room so that his booming voice could be heard throughout the house. In addition, he had a sort of crow's nest installed in the top floor from he would conduct business by telephone. In order to survive the hot New Orleans' summers, in the days before air conditioning, he had built a screened porch where the family could sleep during the sweltering nights. And to remind him of his successes, he kept a stem of bananas hanging. The home, now in possession of Tulane University and home of its president, is an appropriate locale for galas and the ever-necessary fund raisers.

In addition to doing so much for Tulane University, he also founded a chair of English studies at Radcliff college. At Harvard, he founded a chair of anthropology and in New York City the New School or Social Research. He also sponsored the Boston Symphony.

After his son's death in World War Two while serving in the Army Air Corps, he turned his attention to helping the European Jews. His financial assistance had to be given undercover to keep it hidden from British authorities who had instituted a blockade of Palestine and who he dared not offend because of his business interests. He managed to get papers issued, money made available, and ships purchased to help 37,000 Jews settle in Palestine between 1946 and 1948.

Throughout his philanthropy for so many causes he avoided having any of his efforts named after himself.

References:

Cohen, Rich. *The Fish That Ate the Whale.* New York: Picador, 2012.

Fonseca, Mary. *Louisiana Gardens.* Gretna, LA: Pelican,1999.

Hadari, Ze'ev Venia and Ze'ev Tsahor. *Voyage to Freedom: An Episode in the Illegal Immigration to Palestine.* Totowa, NJ: Valentine Mitchell, 1985.

"Lancetilla Botanical Gardens." *Mesoamerica Travel*, S.A. 1-2.

Lachoff, Irwin and Catherine C. Kahn. *The Jewish Community of New Orleans.* Charleston, SC: Arcadia Publishing, 2005.

Malo, Simon. *El Zamorano: Meeting the Challenge of Tropical America.* Melbourne, Australia: Sinbad Books, 1999.

"Samuel Zemurray, American Entrepeneur," *Britannica-Biography, 2016,* 1-6.

"The Philanthropy of the Banana King," *Nonprofit Spotlight: Circles USA,"* 1-3.

"Zemurray Foundation Helps Children," *Fsjna.org, 1-11.*

Chapter Five
Americans from Everywhere

When thinking of Americans south of the border—including Central Americans and South Americans-- often encounter ignorance as to their origins. They are considered mostly of Spanish or of Native Indian American blood or a mixture thereof.

Many people think that all Central and South American countries have remained composed like that forever and there have never been any other people coming into their midst to make any significant changes in the culture.

The many kinds of people living in the United States can be found in all of the regions of the Americas—from all parts of the world and of the many kinds of races, religions, and economic levels. Many United States citizens are only familiar with the hard-working persons known as mestizos-- that is of the mixed Native Indian and Spanish combination. When a Caucasian mentions that he is indeed from countries below the border and is a Hispanic or Latino, many Americans may remark, "You wouldn't pass."

Such an incorrect perception of what a Hispanic look is like is unfortunately commonplace among United States citizens. Names of merchants, managers, and other business types such as Ching, Larach, Craniotis,Wiesenblut, Wienberg, Prouse, Swofford, Cox, Hoffman, and Patti are illustrative of the range of nationalities contributing to the melting pots of countries of the hemisphere going south.

I particularly liked as young kid the appearance of US national by name of Dotsun. I suppose that was the correct spelling of his name. There are people who get irritated when their name begins to sound like Datsun, the car company. I told my mother that I wanted to be like Mr. Dotsun, a tall man of striking personality. Another US national moved about with a bodyguard. Who would endanger his life or was he afraid of something back home that would bring him back to face some sort of reckoning? Many speculated that some were running away from the IRS. In all the Americas you find adventurers seeking a better life.

Thus it was in Honduras where I was born. People of various origins, races, mixtures of races, of differing ethnic folk customs, and so forth. But above all, enriching the culture with their contributions and making life excellent.

Take my family for example. Among my mother, Alma's, relatives. Her father was from the United States with a last name of Rooks, I was told he was from Kentucky. Her mother's last name was Smith. My maternal grandmother's original name was Mesa and was born in Honduras. Her mother was from Spain with really white skin and deep black hair. My father, Richard Rudolf, and his folks were from Germany. Originally from Eisenach. My Zwez grandfather, also a Richard, was an important director with the mighty German AEG that is now Electrolux and owned by Daimler-Benz. All that, be that as it may, leads me to say that my U.S. grandfather Rooks and his son and my father Zwez and my half-brother, Georges, ended up in Honduras. These two sides of my family never met.

What impelled my maternal grandfather to end up in Honduras I don't know.

He continued going south and died from cancer in Santa Marta, Colombia. My father was born in Berlin, Germany in 1882. He arrived in Texas in 1911 from Switzerland where he had moved. After having his cotton crop destroyed by a hail storm outside of Mercedes, Texas, he heard that the United Fruit Company was paying well for banana plantation overseers and decided it was just the job for him. My half-brother Georges returned to Switzerland after seven years in Honduras. He worked first for the Standard Fruit Company and later for the United Fruit Company in Puerto Castilla until the Panama disease shut it down, then in Tela. My family history points out that many sorts of persons contributed to Honduras' mixtures of all sorts. Americans all.

I live in the United States and like so many other citizens I'm the type of individual appropriate to live here and every right to do so since I, too, of the Heinz 57 barbecue sauce mixture variety. I lived many years in New Orleans a city famous for its gumbo population coming from many points of origin. With toleration and good will the mixed population enjoys its diversity and prospers. All of the Americas have been enriched by people from so many nations who were willing to work hard to improve their surroundings and make a life for themselves and their families. They took the rich culture such as they found it and gave it their own spin. That was the Honduras where I lived from 1939 to 1952 and 1953 to 1958. During 1952-1953 I lived in New Orleans with my sister, Betty, and her in-laws.

Perhaps the fact that where my father located, Mercedes, Texas, near Harlingen, happens to be where people of German origin congregated was the reason he chose to live there. In like manner, persons of Middle Eastern origin appeared in San Pedro Sula, the commercial city of Honduras. These persons became known as "turcos." They first appeared when the Middle East was part of the Turkish Ottoman Empire. They were Lebanese and Palestinian Christians. They became dry goods merchants in San Pedro Sula and even took over car dealerships and also ran a sawmill. They ended up being mighty in business, commerce, industry, banking, and even delved in local civic activities and politics. They now have become thoroughly integrated into the fabric of the country.

The Chinese for their part own grocery stores and restaurants. Once again, native-born Hondurans of historical Amerindian and Spanish ancestry found out that foreigners of a different extraction came and amazingly took over important areas in the fabric of the nation. This to some extent stimulated the ire that the native persons felt towards these "foreign" people. Particularly since they helped additional new immigrants from their regions of the world. They were aided in establishing enriching businesses of their own. Suggestions that they be expelled from Honduras went nowhere since the newcomers had become too powerful and influential.

Approximately five percent of Honduras' citizens are of African origin. They live mostly along the coasts. Many came from West Indian islands as slaves or indentured servants. A large group is the Garifuna. They are descendants of an Afro-Carib population that revolted against British authorities on the island of St. Vincent and were forcefully removed in the 18th. Century to the Honduran Bay Islands and then entered the mainland. Others were sent to Belize. Garifunas are famous for their Louvavagu theatrical presentations and their punta music.

As mentioned before, the banana fruit companies preferred to hire as managers people who spoke English and placed the higher echelons in the hands of persons coming from the United States and other predominantly white countries. The United Fruit Company with its

---

Here is my great grandmother, a lady of clear white complexion and deep black hair. She is of peninsular Spanish origin with a family name of Mesa.

The name means “table,” and the coat of arms displays two small, tables with three loaves of bread on each. But the word “mesa” may also deal with a geographic term referring to a tableland or to a flat-topped mountain. It's most common in Southern Spain.

Madrid, the capital of Spain, stands on the Meseta Central.

A Matias Mesa came to New Spain in 1574. The last name appears in almost all the states of the US.

I can trace part of my ancestry to Spain and to its wonderful characteristics. Thus

I'm a Hispanic not only from Honduras, my country of birth, but also from part of my ancestry.

I'm just another of the Heinz 57 American type with a variety of ancestries in my case: Hispanic from Mesa, German from my father's Zwez, and English Rooks from my grandfather and Smith from my grandmother.

Again, in Honduras of Central America, like in the other Americas, people came to a land seeking opportunities not readily available in Europe and getting away from a continent often at war down through centuries. In the Americas, people from nations that had been enemies now could find peace and hopefully prosperity.

frame of mind preferring English- speaking persons and desiring of having a corps of workers owing their existence to the interests of their employer extended its reach to importing West Indian black workers who were given preferential jobs. Their introduction into Honduras created a backlash. There arose among the majority mestizo population racist literature and cartoons ridiculing these descent workers of Caribbean origin. The Honduran government passed immigration laws in 1929 and 1934 that prevented their introduction into the country. In fact, between 1930 and 1939 hundreds of the workers of Caribbean origin were deported. They left for United States and Canada or returned to the same Caribbean islands from where their ancestors had originated.

The first-generation arrivals kept looking back to a certain extent to the cultures from where they originated. But since the characteristics of the Hispanic countries is so distinct and powerful, the following generations became fully integrated into it. Not only that but even when they themselves moved on, they took their now native culture with them.

References:

Bourgois, Phillipe. *Ethnicity at Work: Divided Labor on a Central-American Banana Plantation.* Baltimore: John Hopkins, 1989.

Chambers, Glenn Anthony. *Race, Nation, and West Indian Immigration in Honduras 1890-1940.* Baton Rouge: Louisiana University Press, 2010.

Crowther, Samuel. *The Romance and Rise of the American Tropics.* Garden City, NY: Doubleday, 1929.

Kepner, Charles David. *Social Aspects of the Banana Industry.* New York: Columbia University Press, 1936.

Chapter Six
What a Change!

Can you imagine a greater change? Someone coming from snowy Switzerland with not a banana anywhere in sight. Maybe not even knowing how a banana tree looked. Did it look like a palm tree--the kind that grows in Southern Europe? Coming to a land not known for its snow. No icicles, no icy walks, no frozen puddles. And no black ice destroying highway traffic. Going to Honduras was not my father's, Richard Rudolf, first move. After all he was born in Berlin, Germany, and eventually ended up in Texas after first living in Switzerland.

He came from an upper middle-class family. His father, another Richard, was a commercial director of the mighty Berlin AEG electric company, a very high position in management. My father saw a parade in Berlin featuring Kaiser Wilhelm II. He did not take his hat off when the emperor passed by. So, someone knocked it off. Maybe even got slapped, in the face. That was enough for my parent to decide to leave Germany.

Off he went to Switzerland after he received his inheritance from his family.

After becoming a citizen, he served in the Swiss Army. It decided that it would have greater mobility if its soldiers rode on bicycles. There was a photo of him standing by one.

Good thing that he had left Germany when he did. The First World War started. Perhaps he would have died like his brother Walter killed in Russia on the Eastern Front.

He decided to start a publishing business with a partner. But that turned out to be a disaster. So, he then left for the United States with was left of his inheritance since Europe was too much with its frequent upheavals and limited opportunities to move up in life.

In Texas, there were wide-open spaces. But a hailstorm destroyed his cotton farm. With the United Fruit Company, he could work as a manager and not have to worry that he would lose money on another investment. The Company was well-organized, and it could pick fine people for managers. The big shots were Americans in the 1940s and 1950s when I lived in Honduras. As mentioned, the hospital where I

My grandmother Emma Smith, possibly Schmidt, is shown in her later years at her home in San Pedro Sula, the main industrial and commercial city of Honduras.

She is seen in this photo using a small umbrella as a parasol. The name of this item comes no doubt from Spanish with *para* meaning "stop" and *"sol"* is the word for "sun."

Before the suntan craze and the bronzed skin, ladies were proud to be fair skinned.

She was a steel lady. She owned a whole lot of one-bedroom homes clustered together within a half a block radius. This was outstanding in a country where women only were generally limited to being married or becoming bar girls.

She and her two daughters, my mother, Alma, and my Aunt Vida, had to go through dangerous times when the Liberal and Nationalist parties stirred up revolutions with rampaging soldiers scouring the land. In the period 1920 to 1923, there were seventeen uprisings with the intention of taking over the central government. My grandmother and her two daughters had to get under the crawl space of a house to avoid being raped or killed by crazed revolutionists.

When the fruit companies made sure that all these revolutionary commotions ceased by installing ruthless dictators as presidents in Central American countries, at least these horrible specters threatening civilian life came to an end.

My grandmother preferred to call my mother Alma, meaning "Soul" even though her first name was Paula, and my aunt Vida, meaning "Life" even though her real name was Vidal. With that in mind, my grandmother Emma wanted to be called "Corazon" meaning "Heart" for a meaningful combination of names. My grandmother also had a son who died from burns as a child.

was born in 1939 was characteristic of the hygienic cleanliness brought about by efficiency and by demanding that hard work provide neatness and success. It was run mainly by American doctors and nurses.

The registered nurses, all women, were lovely persons. They wore prim, starched uniforms. Each was dressed according to the colors of the institutions from where they graduated. And they might even sport a medal or two on their uniforms granted to them from somewhere in recognition of their dedicated duty. They were delightful with their cheerful and proper comportment. With their stiff nurses' caps perched upon their head over their elegantly groomed hair piled high like Gibson girls and their eyes merrily glowing and a wide smile radiantly glistening with melodic reassuring voices. These consoling ladies would soothe the patients with engaging conversation. They were angels of mercy and of angelic semblance besides.

The United Fruit Company was prideful of running its operation with dedication to the latest innovations and agricultural approaches. It also wanted to fully control its operations right down to the smallest details as it operated its world in its totality including the homes of its employees, its headquarters, its hospitals, its out- in- the- country clinics, its railroads, its supply channels including having a ranch near Tela to provide milk and meat to its employees, its commissaries to equip its workers with all sorts of items of clothing and other necessities including having smokehouses to give workers the enjoyment of hams, its fleet of ships, and so forth. Everything was integrated and running smoothly.

Look at what the United Fruit Company had done with its plantations. It had drained swamps—great breeding areas from which came the deadly scourges of malaria, yellow fever, and dengue. These diseases were unfortunately always present and ever ready to make once again to make their deadly appearances. A watchful observation was kept on the nearby jungles. If the spider monkeys started dying from yellow fever it was time for the spraying to start to keep the disease from coming out in its plague form to devastate the human population once again.

The Company had cleared jungles and so provided food and work for the people of the countries of Central America and South America. The workers received higher pay than the comparable peasants who labored in the rest of the country, had free hospitalization, free places to stay in the barracks that were provided with rooms for families, and were able to attend up to six years of free education. They could also get passes to travel on the railroad that the Company owned that would take them to cities like El Progreso, La Lima, San Pedro Sula, and Tela. In addition, the passengers could also continue on to La Ceiba in the area of Honduras owned by the Standard Fruit Company. Or they could transfer to the National Railroad that would take them to Puerto Cortés, the main port on the northern part of Honduras.

As a child I was fascinated by the steam locomotives with their hissing and chugging and their might. Many were built by the Baldwin Porter locomotive works.

And after World War Two the Company acquired some that would have been used if the invasion of Japan had taken place. They were a delight to see and one, the 248, even had a song composed to its glory. The trains would carry the banana stems to port and would bring mail to our home and to the workers living in their sanitary, well-kept barracks.

By contrast the train might pass by the wild cane, mud, and a thatch hut of someone having a hardscrabble time earning a living on subsistence farming. The farm laborers lived in safety since they would be asked to leave if they misbehaved by the authorities who made sure that peace and order were maintained.

In those days, electricity was unknown and of course air conditioning was completely unheard off and refrigeration also unless you obtained kerosene to supply the power. To listen to a radio, you needed batteries. Kitchens stood in their own rooms apart from the living quarters of the field workers who had wood stoves.

A central plantation could be walked to that with power from a generator would provide occasional free movies. To see a film for the first time completely mesmerized someone who had never experienced that treat. Also, at a nearby farm there would be a company commissary where the peasants could go to buy not only basic necessities such as clothing but also the machetes and files to keep them sharp in order to make their living cultivating the banana groves.

Just like in the United States in isolated places itinerant salesmen would get off a train and bring knickknacks and fancy goods for sale. These salespeople would also bring foods not readily available out on the plantations such as cheeses and sausages. In addition, they carried

---

This photo shows grandfather Eugene Rooks and his son. Unfortunately, while mother still lived she only referred to her brother as “my brother,” and I did not have the presence of mind to ask for his name.

My grandfather arrived in Honduras for who knows what reasons. He left Kentucky to go wandering in the Hispanic Americas just like so many other persons who emigrated from the United States rather than lead a settled life in their native land.

My father told me he died from cancer in Santa Marta, Colombia.

fancy items such as ribbons and mirrors to add a measure to the otherwise routine lives of the farm worker's wives. And the men might buy items of their preference like a fancy leather scabbard for their machete or a hat to keep their heads protected from the blazing tropical sun as well as from the drenching rains. Religious people would also visit to bring the good news of the Scriptures to these isolated persons.

So, all in all, the plantations workers did well for their hard work maintaining the farm and harvesting bananas.

They could also eat as many bananas as they wished.

Law and order was maintained by the barely literate police. And in those days the use of illegal drugs was unknown, and their availability was nonexistent. Rotgut rum was readily available, however.

But all the glitters is not gold. And the green copper crystals placed at the foot of the banana plants to protect them from stem rot were pretty. And to bring up another by saying that ignorance is bliss in the face of unrecognizable evil, I was unaware that the constant administration of the lovely copper fungicide crystals would eventually end up poisoning the soil.

Soil conservation and the protection of the health of the workers from chemical were unknown concerns in those days. There was also the wholesale destruction of the environment in order to provide land for the banana plantations. The rich alluvial lands or drained marshy land were eventually exhausted of their nutrients by the banana monoculture. A whole plantation had to be abandoned and other land flattened to continue the banana cultivation once the land was thoroughly contaminated by the dreaded Panama disease that attacked the roots of the banana plant.

Once, while riding behind my father's saddle, we came upon the sight of a dragline pulling up dirt to create a surrounding levee. He told me this was an attempt to flood the land in order to kill the virus. A failed attempt if there ever was one. My father would set out daily to keep watch for banana diseases and to report the extent of damage of high winds that would shred the leaves of the banana plants if they had not proceeded to flatten them outright and thus destroy them. The tropical landscape also suffered through the railways of the Tela Railroad Company that tore their way as they advanced. Again, this was not my concern as a child who was awed when riding on a train whose rail coaches were in close proximity to trees full of howler monkeys who became excited with the approach of the majestic locomotive and its carriages.

The Honduran government as was also an example of the other countries where the United Fruit Company exploited the land and were given territory for its banana plantations with the proviso that railroads were laid out. This did happen. But the Company did so with its business interests in mind so that the railroads would carry the bananas to the ports for export. Poor Honduras ended up being the only country in Central America without a railroad leading to its capitol city, Tegucigalpa.

Once I grew up in understanding, I became aware through my mother, a member of the Honduran Liberal Party, that Honduras was ruled by a ruthless dictator, Tiburcio Carías Andino, the leader of the Nationalist Party, who used whatever methods were necessary to crush any opposition to his rule. Naturally, the Company was all too eager to have him ruling the country. That meant that it could acquire land for its plantations at will, never mind other considerations like equal distribution of arable land with no thought given to the native population who also wanted to cultivate their crops. As it was, the country's peasants were left with no other choice but to scramble to find any piece of land that was left over somewhere. To have the dictator in its pocket meant that the Company could ignore having to pay anything but the minimum of taxes.

All of these concerns were of no interest to me since I was in effect the son of the lord of the manor and riding along with my father through the paths through the banana groves with their giant plants was all that impressed me. My father had attained this level after being a timekeeper for a while. This person, who kept track of how much each plantation worker would get paid, lived in a smaller house on the huge plot of land that also included the much larger home of the overseer that contained the plantation's office on the ground floor. My father still had to keep in mind the plantation's payroll. I remember him and the timekeeper spending endless hours day and night while using a mechanical calculator that my father had reconstructed looking for the few cents that prevented the payroll from balancing perfectly. Under my father's supervision were captains that kept track of the work that each laborer performed after being assigned a task that might be keeping the banana plants' shoots from sapping the strength from the parent plant, fertilizing and preventing disease of the plant, harvesting and carrying the banana fruit on the backs of huge mules, bathing the stems with chemicals in order to preserve the fruit, and, finally, loading the banana stems onto railroad cars for transport to the ports of Tela or Puerto Cortés.

The company with its isolated plantations did try to bring a sense of community to the whole with its magazine Unifruitco. In fact, my brother Georges published in it a short story by the name of "Snipe Hunting." Unifruitco told how the company tried to make life pleasant by letting its managers know of the bowling alley it had installed in La Lima and the equine race track and zoo there. It invited dancing with a band playing Dixieland jazz and lots of food to eat at least once a year for the company management and its professional staff in El Progreso. And it brought out how much fun teenagers had dancing La Raspa. It also enhanced in the eyes of its readers the marvel that the company had with its banana ships. After all it had dozens of them and owned the world's largest private navy in its Great White Fleet that sailed as many as fifty ships at a time with the latest advances in propulsion and navigation as well as comfortable quarters for its passengers. It carried over a million tons of general cargo and about sixty thousand passengers per year in addition to the millions of tons of its bananas and sugar production in refrigerated vessels. It allowed its employees to travel on its ships for free.

Taking everything into consideration, the United Fruit Company was operating an empire headquartered in New Orleans. No doubt about it.

Chapter Seven
To the Manor Born

I came home from the Tela, Honduras's, hospital in a motorcar—that wonder of a car with its steel length stretched out and with wide--open seating and running on railroad wheels. I was born in December 16, 1939. That it happened to be Ludwig van Beethoven's birthday and that the German side of my family hailed from Isenach, Germany, the hometown of Johan Sebastian Bach, bode well for someone who would grow up as a great lover of music and who would lend his bit to church choirs praising the loving generosity of our Lord. The fact that the first music I heard was from the waves of the surf breaking along shore of Tela's bay was indeed a beautiful, pleasant, lulling sound. Many years later my father told me that I was born premature. Being born is always a miracle and even more so if you if you come into the world with insufficient time to prepare to meet the course of life. Certainly, this period of the Twentieth Century and a facility that did not at the time possess all the future advances for preemies made my arrival that much more interesting. But the hospital lay by a splendid beach lined with coconut trees bordering the Caribbean Sea, a water expanse redolent with a legendary lore of a highly adventuring individuals and the warring powers of bygone eras and now in the present ready for the display the present ones in a mighty struggle for civilization since World War Two had started in September of this year.

The fact that the coconut trees were painted white a yard above the lovely cream-colored sand made a visitor realize that the Company that owned it was one that bothered itself in making sure that its operations were carried out with a minute interest for details.

My mother and I were headed home to the banana plantation, Farm 19.

Noticeably, my future home's not having a splendid name like the American antebellum plantations of the Deep South indicated that my future home was a standard item just a functional entity, another cog in the Company empire. Both my mother and father had lived most of their lives, especially my Mom, in the heart of cities. She came from San Pedro Sula, Honduras, the main commercial center of the country and Dad came initially from Berlin, Germany, the capital of that powerful nation.

Photographs show my mother, Alma, her sister, Vida, and by grandmother Emma, dressed like stylish modern flappers in their bobbed hairdos, short skirts, and white hose. And an added embellishment was to be wrapped up in a gorgeous shawl, a manton de Manila. My father appears in a family photograph taken in a high-class apartment owned by my grandfather, another Richard like my father, and an important director of his company, with the males dressed in business suits and the females in flowing white gowns worn at the turn of the century. So their living in a plantation devoid of electricity and isolated from the outside world meant sacrificing a more glamorous past to survive in a home provided by the job security of a prosperous corporation. I was being brought to a wholly developed rural civilization that had been setup for the cultivation of bananas. The plantation home that my father had been allotted was the big one of the two on a section of land distanced from the barracks of the farm works since he had become the overseer. Before that he had been a timekeeper in charge with keeping up with the payroll of the plantation and lived in a smaller house. The overseer's house was built on stilts. The first floor was empty space except for the office and a tack area that held the saddles and the rest of the riding equipment. The second floor was accessed by an outside stairs. Once you ascended you would find an open area occupying the whole front. It was protected by being screened, and to keep the rain out, large canvas awnings would drop down. It contained heavy wooden chairs. Behind this open area, to the right were three bedrooms. Two were windowless since the bathroom occupied the external wall of two and the other was behind the large master screened bedroom also protected by heavy canvas awnings. From the large front open area at its center was another open area that traversed all the way to the back wall of the house. Here you would find the refrigerator and the dining table. Then to the left of this area was one windowless bedroom to the front and next to it was the kitchen with its wood stove, built in cabinets, and work table. None of the walls of the house were insulated. Nor were there any ceiling fans. The furnishings of this home down to the beds and to the plates that we ate from were all lent to us by the Company. This was generous, but also created a dependency. So, when someone retired, in the words of an observer of the situation, "You didn't even own a bed onto fall dead." It was up to make this standard house a home.

As far as material possessions were concerned, my mother had inherited some really attractive bric-a-brac from my grandmother, who had died just before I was born, such as a pair of celluloid elephants. One outstanding item was a huge mirror that stood on the floor. It would create quite a stir when a chicken would face it, and the bird would engage in a fight with its mirror image. She had also obtained several upright steamer trunks in which to store clothes since the house did not have any closets, only chests of drawers.

Since my mother was always highly health conscious, she decreed once I started to crawl that no one would enter the living area of the house with shoes. They had to switch to slippers once inside. My half-brother, Andrew, "Andy," my mother's son, remarked that even the dictator of Honduras would have had to do the same if he ever visited our home.

As I grew to be a bigger baby, a carpenter made for me a rolling walker from fine Honduras mahogany, the best in the world, so that I could pretend to walk or at least push myself along the upper story of the plantation home. Even though I had other siblings, my father's son, my half-brother, Georges, living in Switzerland, Andy off to high school, my father's son, Harry, off on his own, and my sister "Betty" at the United Fruit American Boarding School in El Progreso, Honduras, studying at the elementary school level, all of them were older by at least twelve to fourteen years, I was practically an only child at home and the sole object of attention of my parents. Although I only had half-brothers and a half-sister, they would always throughout the rest of their lives loved me. Even though they were less than perfect, I would also correspond their great love with my own.

My mother thought that I could possibly do well if she entered me in a child beauty contest in San Pedro Sula. I won first prize as an outstanding example of child development. This gave my brother Andy a chance to make the remark, "No wonder you won. You were the only blond!"

But if my parents provided me for me all the benefits, they could possibly give me, our living out in the boondocks of a banana plantation had its drawbacks. Since the Company felt that it had no need to provide for the benefit of electricity for any of its employees on the banana plantation we had none. Everything had to be run like in former pre-Edison inventions days. That meant that we had to have a wood stove. And at night light for the most part had to be provided by kerosene lamps. Kerosene also supplied the power to our refrigerator. So, we made our living as such. Some people like to enjoy the rough, primitive life as campers even sleeping in a pup tent and the like. But there is something in human nature that doesn't appreciate a downgraded life by being forced to live in a lesser status. Thus, to us the fuel kerosene made a big difference. There is the perpetual country music joke of having a kerosene guitar in lieu of an electric one. But the ever so useful kerosene can only help so far.

We also enjoyed the use of the large yard in the back of the farm house with its barrel of gasoline that provided fuel for my father's generator. He could have then electricity so that he could listen to his short-wave radio at night for two hours. Once I was older, it made me wonder what sort of memories went through his mind about his life in Europe while he heard classical music. Once in a while, as a rarity, when he would hear old waltzes his mind could wander off to the days when he enjoyed the company of friends back in the days before he left Germany and Switzerland. He occasionally would tune in on the cowboy music he would pick up coming from the United States so that I would enjoy it. There was a really powerful station that would describe itself by saying that it was coming from Nuevo Laredo in Old Mexico. And then there was an Armed Forces radio for the service people far from home in such places as the bases located at the Panama Canal. My father would have to recourse to lighting with a kerosene lamp when he would awaken during the night around four in the morning and read a while before going back to sleep once again.

Even though my father did not strive to make a musicologist out of me, he did make sure that I acquired a treasure of eternal value: the ability to speak English from the very beginning in a country where Spanish was dominant. Curiously, I got into a habit in speaking in English to my father, my sister Betty, and my brother Harry whenever we would visit him, and I spoke in Spanish to my mother and my brother Andy.

My mother busied herself with running the home and raising corn in areas not devoted to banana plantings. With the money coming from the sale of this grain she was able to send her son and my half- brother

Andy to Belize, then the capital of British Honduras in the country now called Belize. There he attended a high school run by

Anglican clergy. He also picked up English with a Caribbean accent and laughed as he learned some Belize Kriol with its unique treatment of the language. For instance, I was told that "Mecago to de baha cha" meant "I'll go to the barber shop." And somewhat lengthy words like "Yarborough" would be streamlined to "Yabra."

My father objected to my mother choosing unused Company land to raise corn.

But since the Company did not pay him enough to send my brother away to school my mother decided that her action was necessary and must proceed. She had no other choice since my father never made more than $165.00 a month and that was what he was making when he retired in 1953. Since the Company provided him with everything in the way of housing, hospitalization, travel, servants, and cheap food it paid him a bare minimum. Raising the corn crop had a specific problem as it was grown in a tropical country. It was subject to attack from parakeets. If the little birds would have been satisfied by eating from a few corn pods, it wouldn't have been so much of a problem. But the attackers had to mess over the whole field and wreck a whole lot of ears of corn. So, a kid had to be stationed to repel their invasions and consequent damage with a slingshot. A scarecrow no longer kept them away. It was a shame to try to kill off as many of these cute little monsters when they became destroyers of human food.

When the corn harvest came in, I was delighted how the harvesting proceeded.

After the corn had been removed from the husk, then it was time to shell corn. Since we had no electricity my mother had to resort to a hand operated corn sheller. It was fun to watch it operate as the corn would jump out and land in a pile separated from the cob.

The kernels look so pretty as little golden gems. It was a delight to dig my little hands into this treasure throve. Was I delighted as I grew older to take note of how a little grain of corn would produce a stalk of corn with several ears of grain! Then after the harvest the corn would be changed into tortilla meal once it lost its shell after being soaked in a quicklime solution. My mother, once in a while, would make out of cornmeal dough an additional culinary marvel, excellent Honduras tamales. The cornmeal would be readied with lard. Mom would the enrich the cornmeal's content by inserting small hunks of meat either chicken, beef, or pork, and chickpeas, raisins, and olives in generous amounts. The whole loaf would be wrapped in banana leaves and boiled. The transformation would yield a meal of marvelous flavors.

My family also had a cook and a maid and a yard man who lived in a little apartment building in the back of our huge yard. The man kept our grass cut with one of the push mechanical lawn mowers and chopped wood for our wood stove. In the back yard of our plantation home there was a large chicken coop. My mother greatly enjoyed having a hen hatch additional chicks. Mom would even go to the trouble of bringing the hen's nest into the house and aid the chicks as they struggled to get out of their egg shells. I loved to see them to come to life in such a magical fashion. I loved watching the chickens eat when I tossed feed at their feet. Later I would watch them as they would supplement their diet with scratching the ground and grass for whatever they could find. But, also, they would relax as they took dust baths. Also, of interest seeing how the roosters carried their love approach to the hens. And consequently, the hens going to their nests in the hen house to lay their eggs. After hatching them the hens would run around with their flocks of chicks and sit with the brood under their wings. As highly defensive mothers, the hens would attack and chase off a dog that approached even though it might be much bigger. The chickens and their ways of living were interesting as were their sounds such as those made by the hens clucking as they celebrated the laying of another egg, the roosters crowing, and the low warning screech if they saw a predator flying overhead such as a hawk.

We enjoyed the fresh eggs. And to further encourage the egg laying my father placed fake eggs made out of plaster of Paris in the nests.

The chickens provided us with their delicious flesh. My mother could do a great job cooking fried chicken. She was sure to make some when the American superintendents came to visit the farm to speak with my father concerning the banana plantation's management I looked forward to eating a chicken gizzard. But a rascal was cheating me. I was informed that a rooster had no gizzard. This was a barefaced lie since both hens and roosters must have gizzards as part of their digestive systems.

Who in my family was cheating me out of my delicacy? But being a kid who was ignorant and willing as an innocent to believe just about any lie, I was taken in by this deceit. I was not only until many years later that I realized that I had been duped. To think that one my beloved family members had been deceiving me! When I arrived at the United States as a teenager in 1952, I went to a supermarket and found out that whole packets of gizzards could be bought. I felt that I had died and gone to Heaven!

My father tried to be a good provider, and he sought how to take full advantage

of the environment he found himself as part of the empire of banana production of the United Fruit Company. For instance, he noticed that the banana plants produced a lot of flowers and that bees helped to pollinate them. So, he decided he would go into bee keeping. He constructed boxes made out of wood with frames that could be inserted and pulled out. The frames had wires inside where the bees could attach the wax cells that held the honey as well as the bees' reproduction cells. Dad would pull out the frames not only to extract the honey but also to keep watch for intruders who would try to invade the beehive and take advantage of it. For example, my father might find eggs that had been laid by a wasp within the beehive. He not only deprived the bees of their honey, but he was also their protector. It was a delight to watch the bees flying in and out of the wooden hives looking like emerging golden gems created seemingly out of the gold tropical sunlight. It was interesting and amusing to see my father don a head covering with a mesh screen to protect himself from bee stings as well as thick gloves while blowing smoke from a tin dispenser to cause the bees to become sleepy and calm down.

What a joy it was to savor the honey while it was still imbedded in the wax cells. And after the honey had been extracted to enjoy it with pancakes. My father would mold the wax from the beehive into flat, round cakes for storage.

In addition to the bees there were a myriad variety of hummingbirds also enjoying the nectar of the flowering bushes as part of the creation of the vast, seemingly never ending beautiful ingenuity so characteristic of the tropical creativity They also looked like jewels, especially when the sunlight would strike their iridescent bodies.

More feathered beings appeared in the presence of a variety of colored parrots and macaws whose friendliness you had to be on guard not to abuse lest a sharp beak would remind you that familiarity has its limits. But with increasing approaches, one of them would eventually wrap its talons around one of your fingers or wrists. One of the wings had to be shortened lest they decide to leave and prefer the wild and its liberty rather than continue to enjoy the handouts from humans that brought captivity as its cost. Our favorites were the yellow-headed parrots that would speak and even learn a short song. How extraordinary was to watch these birds express their excitement by strutting about while making sounds and doing the amazing controlled contractions and expansions of their pupils. As expected with the seemingly endless tropical variations were so many more bird species including the quetzal with their long tail feathers so favored in the outfits of the ancient Mayas. And, of course, the great gamut of colorations, especially the brilliant tones of the toucans' large beaks. And not to be left out, there were the larger but dull colored birds such as the chachalacas and the black, majestic-looking great curassows. But the tropical aviary is not to be forgotten after sunset. When I my father would turn on his kerosene lamp to read around four in the stillness of night, you could hear birds serenading with such participants as the screeches of the owls and the melodic songs of the tropical mockingbirds that might decide to sing throughout in spite of the darkness.

If the air of the tropical skies were populated with such a variety of species so it was also true at ground level. In my early years I was to learn the Spanish names of the many distinctive denizens that nature had provided as I became increasingly aware of my richly blessed surroundings.

They ranged with the brownish furred little animals: guatuzas (agoutis), pisotes (coatimundis), tacuazines (possums), olingos (racoon-like), cusucos (armadillos), javelinas (peccaries) like little hairy pigs as well as the large dull-colored dantos (tapirs) with snouts reminiscent of those of elephants. Such a striking

menagerie running around about at ground level. The native people would capture any number of these creatures in order to eat them. A big tapir would feed a good deal of people. But the javelinas would be as welcome as having pork. But it was said that certain glands needed to be removed or they would spoil the killed flesh. I once had ham made out of boar flesh. I have never eaten a tastier one.

Danger lurked with the great variety of snakes including the deadly barba amarilla (fer-de-lance) and the colorful black, yellow, and red banded coral snake. It certainly looks like a pretty necklace. Good thing that as toddler I didn't meet up with one and decided to pick it up and play with it as if it was just another living creature to keep as a pet. It is hard to imagine but there was the story of people keeping a rattlesnake as a pet. Certainly, to have it and make it shake its rattle at will would be interesting. A song mentioned having one and having tied a golden ribbon near its head.

But there was no need to run into a snake. Most likely when meeting up with a human it would take it as another predator and would slink off as least as fast as the scared person.

If one dared to cross one of our yards or even get on a slab of concrete, our yard man would slam his razor-sharp machete on it. It would never cease to amaze me that the separated pieces would continue to scamper about.

There were more than enough reptiles with territorial ambitions ready to make their presence known and ready to hold their ground with deadly intentions. So, it was nice to have other creatures with scaly skins, the lizards that were harmless. It was nice that there could be large ones, some close to weighing ten pounds called iguanas. The ones we were acquainted with were green ones although not completely so since they also could have orange and blue colored areas. It was great to hold their soft bodies in your hands and not worry that would try to harm you. They looked so much like small dragons that they were a thrill to see how much they resembled those fabulous creatures and yet they were happy enough just to shake their heads even they were eager enough to scamper away with their undulating bodies or running off straight ahead with their tails up in the air. As much as I loved the iguanas, I wasn't looking forward to eating the fleshy tails of these "tree chickens." Nor did I follow my father's example of sucking on their leathery eggs. And he enjoyed them raw! Yuck!

What if a giant reptile came calling? There could be invaders looking to exert with their huge bodies their desire to get their way by throwing their weight from a branch. One night my father and all of the rest of us became aware of the loud screeches coming from the chicken coop at night. Sure enough there was cause for alarm. A boa constrictor was hanging from a nearby tree with its slit eyes gawking at the chickens that it would like to have as its next meal. Dad make quick work of its invasion. One shot from his one-shot shotgun killed it. What about getting it down from the tree now that it was dead? No need to be concerned about it. Let it rot as it remained entangled in the tree branches. Besides, it became the interest of buzzards with their the ugly, black, bald heads, and necks. It was amazing to see them flying effortless up high as they coasted along with the warm air currents. I knew all about their aerobics since as a constantly inquisitive child I would have found out through the constant stream of question I sent forth to my father who invariably would answer each question graciously even when I let go with a barrage of them.

I heard of airplane pilots who took devilish glee of going at the flying buzzards and cutting them up with the plane propellers. What a mess it must have made on the windshields! But obviously evil minds don't worry about such trivia.

But going back to the snakes, it was a fact that snakes to some were another way to make a meal. Or get other products from the carcass. A boa like the one my father killed that was nicely plump round and like ten feet long had a lot of fat that could be used in many ways, one of them being using it as a balm for a sore muscle or rubbing some on a healing wound so as not to have it become tight.

The insect world had many wonders. Such as their splendid beauty. There was a butterfly that flew with transparent wings that looked like they were made of cellophane. The leaf cutter ants seen carrying tremendous loads were a wonder. Even greater amazement resulted when you found out that the big pieces in contrast to the small size of the ants were being carried underground to fertilize fungus gardens. Such a genius gift nature had given to them!!

And I hate to mention the ticks and others that were ready to jump on you at the least opportunity. My dear mother was scared that while she was pregnant with me might develop malaria from an infected mosquito bite. So, she fed herself a sustained stream of Atabrine tablets. The mosquitos were a constant threat since besides malaria, they could sicken human beings with dengue and yellow fever. The Company would start wholesale spraying so as to control the insects. It knew that when the monkeys started to die from these diseases it was time to start spraying.

The monkeys figured that they owned the jungle. The jungle was formed by either land being held in reserve to be converted to banana plantations once it became infected with the dreaded banana diseases and was allowed to lie fallow back to jungle and recover its former format.

The monkeys were a treat to watch as a passenger train would wind its way through the jungle. They would go into paroxysms of wild frenzy jumping through the branches of huge trees. They were as much fun as watching a circus act. The jungle itself is a treasure chest of wonderful woods. It provides mankind with the famous Honduras mahogany beautiful lumber. The tropical climate provides so many delicious fruits such a avocados, mangoes, guavas, and papayas. Besides, there are others less popular to Americans such as guanabanas and sapotes. The strangest tasty fruit, if it can be called such are the carao pods. They are woody and must be hammered open to reveal cells on whose walls there are dabs of jelly-like sweet substance. Tropical nuts called coyoles are in a very tough kernel that also have to be hammered open. While cashew nuts are well known in the United States, people are not aware that it comes beneath a fruit called the cashew apple. All these tasty products of nature grow in abundance under the tropical sun and copious rainfall for all to enjoy both humans and the animal kingdom. The fruits are of great nutritional value and even provide medicinal properties.

Besides humans what is at the top of the food chain? We have to take into account the big cats of the Americas, the puma also known as a cougar or mountain lion and the even bigger jaguar.

The parrots, macaws, and monkeys drawn from our jungle surroundings were a lot of fun to enjoy as they were provided with fruits and insects in a very great variety and abundance by the generous tropical biology. Not to mention the rich majesty of the jungle settings including its rich foliage and in particular the enormous ceiba trees one of which we treasured as it rose majestically above the cleared area so that we could gaze on it from our main bedroom window. In addition, the plantation's environment had the availability of horses and dozens of mules to enjoy riding, even though these were more often beasts of burden available to carry the stems of bananas to the waiting railroad cars that would transport them to ocean-going ships.

Being that humans tend to be social, there were also managerial employees and their wives including those who taught at the American schools of the Company. My mother would stay in touch with the Company wives through the use of our wall telephone with its protruding mouthpiece and hanging receiver. Depending on how many yanks you gave to the side crank, it would connect her with whichever party she wanted to call. Going crazy with the crank connected you with everyone. I would get into the act by her allowing me to sing on the phone Dr. Ross's pills commercial jingle. Years later I was telling a radio commentator about this singing. He then made the remark, "But Richard has not told us how many times they hung up on him!"

We had a great life on the plantation although it had the drawbacks of a primitive life without electricity. But all in all, we had elements that made us feel that we were enjoying rich lives. We were not financially wealthy but as the saying goes, "We were poor, but we didn't know it."

Chapter Eight
Life Everywhere

Banana trees grew by the thousands in the plantation. My father's job was to see that it prospered. He would set out on his horse and inspect the plantation. It was a delight to see my dad come riding back home after having inspected his domain. As my life took hold and I became a little boy, I was able to ride behind his saddle as he made his rounds. But first I had to get large enough to do so. So, one day when my father came riding into the grounds of the plantation home I took every stitch of my clothing off. I stood out with my little body proudly displayed in the bright daylight. That did get my father's attention, and he made a favorable comment at my bodily performance.

I was so glad that my father was my dad. He was a wonderful parent. Of course, I would only know him as a gray-haired man. He had been born in 1884 in Berlin. He was so very loving and patient. To have me as a little child in his increasing years was obviously, something of pride to him.

Even with his increasing years he managed to stay healthy. He was fair with blue eyes. The tropical sun did not spare him. The fair skin on his arms took a beating as he wore short sleeve shirts. In those days people knew nothing about sunscreens. The skin of his arms turned black. A man with lesser life force in him would have contracted melanoma cancer and on a grand scale. While it was true that his blackened arms bled a lot easier if he scratched them, he was free from cancer throughout his life.

Back around the middle of the Twentieth Century people were not subject to a lot of scientific scares. They lived on without a care about cholesterol. Heck, cooking with lard was all the rage. Nor did scientists do battle with each other with one group claiming one opinion and another contradicting the former. Coffee drinking, for example, some blame it for declining health while others in the scientific community take the opposite view. Heck, even lard that was accused with clogging people's veins and arteries now has admirers that laud its nutritional values. In our home there was lots of coffee drinking. After all, I was in a land that grew coffee and its cultivation was another natural product that contributed to the economy of the nation.

Our kitchen also used hydrogenated oil for cooking. The solid product was a bright white product so it was no wonder that it labeled itself as La Blanquita. This kind of cooking product also was charged with having unhealthy tendencies leading to cancer among other horrifying consequences. But we managed to do well. My father was healthy and so was the rest of the family. I look so longingly to this past moment of my life when all of my beloved family members were still all alive and none in the hospital.

So, my father was in charge of having the banana trees prosper and produce large, wholesome fruit. And the looks of the fruit required careful cultivation. An agronomist must have been hired by the Company to do research as to which fertilizers worked best, and which chemicals could possibly ward off plant disease.

As with any plant, the banana requires watering. Even in tropical areas there can have torrential rains for days at a time but a dry spell could come along. So Sam Zemurray, keeping his eyes on any problem in his plantation empire, came up with a solution on how to deal with the droughts. He spent a great deal of money installing high above the banana plants aerial sprayers. And to have the pressure to spray the water and create this artificial rain he spent another ton of money bringing in huge pumps capable to do the job. I remember looking at a pump on the plantation that was so huge that it had a walkway around its sides. Outside of the shed that held this monster there would be pools of oil. My father, always conservative with money and always thinking of how to save funds would advise me to dip my leather shoes into the oil so that, according to his thinking, my shoes would last longer and besides they would become waterproof. But by the time I was growing up, I became maybe a little wary of my father's far-flung advice I deferred to a later time, so to speak, following this bit of wisdom. Oily socks could be among other possible problems.

Each plantation where we resided had a few differing characteristics – Dad would be moved from one farm to another from time to time-- one timekeeper's house had a large bamboo grove at its back. The timekeeper's cook took some of the excess embers from the wood stove and threw them too close to it. Some of the dry bamboo leaves on the perimeter ignited and the fire from them raced into the bamboo grove itself. When the fire really got going it was scrambling for every iguana to save itself. And they came streaming out by the dozen. That certainly was a sight to see! But, of course, these splendid outbursts were rare. Nature could make itself felt with single threatening appearances as in the case of a boa that was left to rot as it died twisted around the limbs of a tree.

My father was neither a hunter nor a fisherman. But there was game to be hunted and fishing did take place in the mighty Ulua River that not only had plentiful fish but also provided much needed water for the overhead irrigation system. Dove hunting was something that my brother Andrew engaged in with his .22 rifle. And he did kill quite a few of the light brown birdies. But a firearm is also dangerous if not treated with care. And as the old saying has it, if you play with fire, you're liable to get burned.

So, one day my brother managed to shoot himself in the upper leg with his rifle. A doctor said that he came mighty close to severing an artery with the shot. If so he would have bled to death. As it was, he lived on, but one would hope a more careful hunter with his rifle. The farm workers would also engage in hunting. Evidence of that were the skins of deer and an occasional jaguar. What really provided a lot of edible meat were the tapirs. These miniature elephants were famous for being well filled out with their rotund bodies. Thus, they had lots of flesh to offer. But oftentimes when such a hunting treat was not available a human being would have to make do with a humble armadillo or opossum.

My mother really liked this photograph of herself. She is shown wearing a capeline hat at a stylish angle worn at the height of fashion in the nineteen thirties The hat is seen as being light and airy.

So the cloche close-fitting hat that the flappers often wore was not the only head gear prominent at this time.

In the hot tropics the capeline hat would have been so much more appropriate.

The photo was hand tinted to bring out the redness of the lips and the blue of the dress as well as the delicate pink of the roses decorating the hat.

My mother always liked to stay up with the fashion styles of the day. She allowed me to appreciate the allure of a well-dressed lady.

As a person at ease and lighthearted, she made many friends and was welcome to stay in lady friends' homes wherever she went. She managed to retain her friends despite the confining situation of having to live on a banana plantation away from city life.

This photograph was taken before she became my father's wife and was drawn into the the scheme of things of the Company.

So as the daughter of a mother that could provide well for her, she shows that she was of comfortable means before she married my father.

It also demonstrated that my mother, her sister, and their mother could be well-off without having to depend on any Fruit Company for their prosperity.

What can be more beautiful than a baby photograph?

It shows the product brought about by the love of two people.

That's a look of trust that its needs will be taken care off.

It shows a feeling that its cries for help will be answered with tender love.

Now it demonstrates that its entry into the world is welcome.

It holds the promise that a way is open for it to form a part of humanity.

Loving people hope that its future will be happy.

Down through the ages this being has succeeded into a new generation.

This mortal only knows of life and of continuing to exist.

It shows the desire of the world that people should go on to the next generation.

Its smile is of innocence not tainted by the world's corruption.

Those around it hope that its entry is a blessing to all.

Humanity hopes that it will choose a path of righteousness.

One hopes that faith in God will light its way.

Continuing that baby's smile throughout life should be a supreme goal of existence.

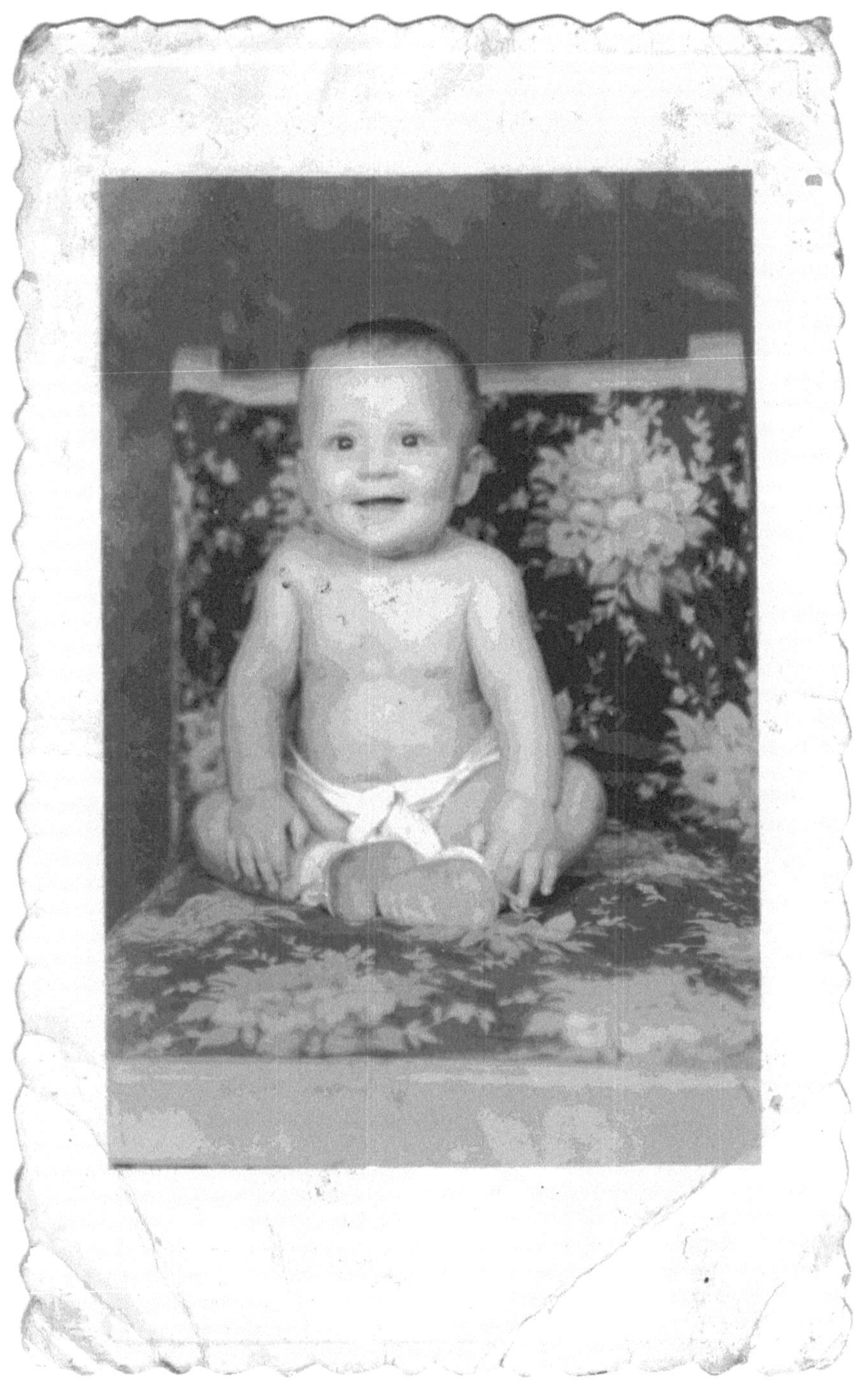

My sister Elizabeth, always known as "Betty," is holding me so that my photograph will be taken with her.

The way she is holding me and the way my eyes are shut and my legs are buckled as well as my sister's somewhat strained look seems to indicate that she is having a rough time holding me so that our joint picture shall be taken.

The photograph does illustrate the loveliness of my sister and the beauty of her love for me, hard as it might be at times to gain my cooperation.

She was like a second mother to me, and the affection that we shared was truly wonderful and continued on for the many years when we were close geographically.

This photo is also significant because the background of this shot shows a railroad freight car used to transport the bananas from our plantation that at this time would be Farm 19.

The composite feeling of this photograph is of our life on the plantation and the means that sustained our existence.is period allow me to learn something of the country in which I lived besides just the American culture of the Company.

This is a funny photograph but not because of my concerned expression and my father's attempt at making me understand what is going on with the photographer and his purpose.

It is humorous because of my bewilderment at something going on that is harmless and is on the contrary, beneficial.

It wasn't meant to be a trick shot. But our dog decided to park itself directly behind my father with its legs showing just at this very moment. This led my mother to say, “Your Dad came out with all six legs showing!”

The photographer who took the picture of my sister Betty and me and as well as this one was most probably an itinerant one like so many other merchants who came to visit the plantation in search of making some extra dough.

Someone told me--with who knows what truth there was to it--that the way my mother met my father was when her mother and she came to a plantation that my father was supervising and were selling items to the farm laborers. My mother was flustered at this revelation and was disdainful that she and her mother would stoop to do this.

The photograph is a good one of my father. At the time he was in his early sixties and still in great health. I was blessed that my Dad was a mature man and not some young fellow who was still wet behind the ears.

The great care I was given is seen in the little sailor outfit I'm wearing. No one was thinking at the time that the day would come that I would indeed become a sailor in the United States Navy.

This photograph if one of a set. The other one shows me standing up. But this one was the one chosen by the newspaper telling about my being the winner of a children's municipal contest at the Main City Festival of San Pedro Sula, the commercial and industrial capital of Honduras.

The caption under the newspaper photograph mentioned that I was chosen because of my healthy and well-developed physique. I'm also all dolled up in an elegant outfit.

It does display me much more at ease than the pictures taken with my sister and my father.

My brother Andrew remarked at my success, "No wonder he won. He was the only blond in the lot." My hair was done up in curls, and my sister Betty claims that she was the one that took care of that, not surprisingly since she was like a second mother to me.

Curiously, while my mother was pregnant, she wished that I would be a girl. She was all set to name me "Sweetheart". But, alas, she had another son.

She told me that I came out yellow when I was born because she took Atabrine, a medicine used to prevent malaria. But was that the reason I was that color? A lot of babies come out a little jaundiced anyhow.

I don't look skinny as I did in the previous two photos. That meant that I had survived without vaccinations since none were available in our plantation setting not to mention the many tropical diseases lurking about.

This photograph shows my mother's first child, my brother Andrew, known as “Andy.”

My brother Georges, known as “George,” was the result of my father's first marriage to a Jewish lady from Romania. My sister’s full name Gladys Elizabeth, so she told me, was known as “Betty” and my brother Harry were children born out of my father’s marriage to a Honduran lady.

Andrew as seen looks like a thorough cowboy in his outfit. Lest anyone mistake him as a poor fake, he is displaying full regalia including chaps. And in his eagerness to show that he means business, he brandishes his six-shooter.

The photo illustrates the great influence that United States culture had in Honduras. When I was a boy, I loved western movies. I couldn’t get enough then. And I enjoyed with anticipation the onscreen exploits of the various actors who portrayed themselves as the heroes upholding decent life against the marauding desperadoes who preyed on the stagecoaches and arrived at western towns ready to shoot anyone who got in their way.

Andrew's father was the owner of a prosperous car repair shop not dependent on Company business, and he sired many brothers and sisters for my brother. Thus, his father was certainly rich enough to provide Andy with the swaggering attire that he so boldly displays.

This photograph shows me with my mother and my cousin Teodora, called “Yoya.”

Yoya, the eldest of my Aunt Vida's three daughters, is probably why she was chosen to take a picture with the two of us.

The photo was probably taken at Puerto Cortes, the port where my Aunt Vida and her husband Luis Murillo resided.

We would go visit our relatives in Puerto Cortes from time to time, and they had even come to visit us at the banana plantation.

It was a great idea on my mother’s part to introduce me to the rest of my family in a city. My extended folks added an additional dimension to my life. It carried me away from the limited exposure I had to people by living exclusively on the plantation.

Puerto Cortes was the main banana shipping port for the Tela Railroad Company branch of the United Fruit Company.

Like the port of Tela with its company wharf facilities, there was a Company side to Puerto Cortes called “Campo Rojo,” or Red Camp. with its large hotel and fine dining.

Beyond this American area there was a place called “El Faro,” which really wasn't a lighthouse but was a suspended lookout for German submarines during WWII.

Chapter Nine
Needs

The battle to maintain its profitability was always paramount for the United Fruit Company that had, like all companies, to please its investors. It was intent in cutting costs wherever it could. It also kept possible competitors away. One way was to be sure that there was peace and security where it operated. In Honduras a dictator's name was Tiburcio Carías Andino, simply known as Carías. He was one of Central America's dictators with El Salvador having Maximiliano Hernández Martinez and Nicaragua's Anastacio Somoza Debayle. They made sure that the Company's interests were preserved against any opposition that reared up demanding higher wages, better working conditions or redistribution of land so that the native population could grow crops after the Company's desire for total land grab. This conclave of dictators led to their countries, with their overwhelming willingness to cooperate with the Company, to be called "Banana Republics."

If by some miracle a population created labor trouble for the Company, it would move its operations somewhere else and remove, raze, and destroy all buildings, their facilities, and means of production and leave the people without the means of sustenance.

Poorly educated policemen dressed in khaki uniforms and pith helmets and carrying Mauser rifles created an atmosphere of intimidation.

Carías had founded the National Party, and he had been promoted to general through his continuing participation in one revolution after another. Carías was a massive man. At six foot, two inches tall he towered over his countrymen. He had a huge head with drooping cheeks, hooded eyelids, and a downward mustache covering his whole upper lip. He was also obese, and his huge bulk led his detractors to calling him "La Buchona," translated as "The Blubbery" with a change of gender right along. He would brook no opposition, and he had his goons to enforce his will. One of them was known as "Caquita" translated as "Little Shit." He got his name by giving troublemakers a good dosage of castor oil. Or someone stirring trouble would be made to do a hundred sit ups or get beat up. If need be, Carías would become ruthless. It was a common rumor that he had his own private cemetery. The political opposition still remained as best as it could and hoped to surge up someday and have a democratic government freely elected without the threatening intervention of the military. When one went into the cities you would notice that stencils had been used to portray Carías on building walls with the sarcastic slogan of "The Founder of Democracy." Sometimes, someone would place a lighted cigarette by a large firework set to go off when a night patrol of Carías' gangsters was going about to rattle them.

Zemurray showed his dark side by lending his support to the Central American dictators. And the politicians in Washington were known to remark about any of the dictators, "He is a bastard, but he is our bastard."

Since my grandmother and my mother were outspoken member of opposition Liberal Party they were bound to suffer. During one of the past revolutions my grandmother's house was looted. My mother told me that one time when revolutionists were rampaging my grandmother, Emma, and her two daughters, including my mother, Alma, and her sister, Vida, having to hide in the narrow crawl space under one of the houses they owned. They could not sneeze despite of the dust, or they would have been in a world of trouble. Since my mother, Alma, was a member of the Liberal Party I was well aware of the state of politics in Honduras and the criticism thereof.

My father was well aware of the pitiful political conditions in Honduras, but he kept his mouth shut. He certainly couldn't afford to lose his job, especially as he grew to be an old man.

My father who had come to Honduras because of a good salary and a whole raft of benefits found that the pay wasn't keeping up with inflation. True, Dad didn't have to worry with the costs of owning a car, didn't have to pay a mortgage or pay rent, got cheap food, free medical care, free transportation on trains and if he wanted, he could to go on the banana ships that had cabins for passengers, and so forth. The free train and trips extended to his immediate family. But cash on hand could be a problem. He had three children he needed to take care of beside him and my mother. They needed to acquire an education. The company schools provided just basic education and on the banana farms where he was employed there was no school education available for us.

So this was not a problem as long as my brother Andy was in Belize as a boarding school student and my sister Betty attended middle school as a boarding student at Progreso American School. But my father had to save for the future when my mother would have to leave the plantation and take all three of us to San Pedro Sula for our educations. The fact that my father had to economize for our future education was the reason I never was able to get a tricycle as much as I begged. But my father would get me a small toy once in a while when he would go to the city with me or by himself. Unfortunately, sometimes I had the habit of taking apart a mechanical toy such as one run by a spring to see how it worked. I had few toys. One day I found out that some were missing. I questioned about it and found out that Dad had given them to the poor farm workers' children. I was beyond livid with rage. He could have spent his money and bought some for them!

My father due to his low income was very economical with himself. He had just a few clothes and his only real pleasures in our home was listening to his shortwave radio at night and reading magazines such as Life, Time, Popular Mechanics, and Science Digest. He also enjoyed writing to my brother in Switzerland, Georges, who was doing well and was an inspiration to all in the family. He, like my father, could speak English, German, French, and the Spanish he learned during his stay with Dad in Honduras. Also, this brother could speak these languages with their correct accents.

In addition, my brother living in a multilingual country could speak in addition Italian and Switzerdeutch—the German dialect spoken in Switzerland. His ability with languages aided him as he traveled to the countries of Europe selling precision tools.

As such he was a traveling salesman who sold Swiss machinery famous for its quality including automatic lathes that would copy a piece of machine by the use of sensors. He married a secretary of a place where he worked whose father was a Calvinist minister of some financial means. So, he was a member of the family worthy of emulation as a member of the family who was a model of what we could achieve.

Unbeknownst to my child's mind the days were drawing near when I and my two remaining at-home siblings would have to leave our tropical garden of Eden and transfer to city life. Gone would be the happy times of living s sheltered life as well as the sweet company of my parents. After all, with my siblings gone I had a monopoly on their affections. True, before I left to go to the school in the big city, I wasn't a complete ignoramus. Through my mother, I had grown well acquainted with the wondrous music of Hispanic people. Honduras was the repository of music coming from all over the Hispanic world with beautiful waltzes of the upper crust as well as rhythms such as tangos, rhumbas, congas, ballads, and boleros arising from common folks of varied origins and ethnic groups. The ranch type ballads accompanied by mariachi bands were especially notable for us since they spoke of life with horses and country life similar to ours not to mention the exaltation of the Mexican revolution.

The workers at plantation were fine musicians and at the distance of my father's and the dwellings you could hear their guitar playing and singing at about a quarter mile away in the very deep stillness of a country night. The peasants of the plantation also had their fun. Once a year they would put on hideous masks and go around begging while poking fun at Judas, the infamous betrayer of Jesus. The plantation workers could also enjoy city life when they would get free train passes to go to El Progreso, which was also a train junction to various places in the northern part of Honduras. In El Progreso, they could buy goods and get dental work done and also get good and drunk as well as enjoy fleshy pleasures at the cantinas.

Our family also had to go to El Progreso for dental work or rely on someone out in the country with limited dental expertise. I recall there was a time I was having trouble with a molar. Being the brat I was, I refused having the man look into my mouth. So, he got me talking and while I had my mouth open, he jumped on me all of a sudden and extracted my tooth without any dental anesthesia.

On the farm there was no medical care. You could get along buying over-the-counter medications such as aspirins and milk of magnesia. Otherwise, you had to ride on a horse to a distant company dispensary. On hand were medications intended for the mules and horses such as liniment for their muscular soreness and a tar-like substance called creosote; it was used as an antibiotic. The liniment intended for beasts of burden could also be used on humans for muscular soreness and when I suffered from earache my father would administer with a dropper drops of it down my ear canal. And the tarry substance would be applied to human skin infections as well as treating dog sores and the mange. We believed in treating our animals with the best of care possible including those taken from the jungle such as parrots and monkeys. My mother believed in making the most of our isolated plantation situation. She easily made friends including getting to know the plantations managers' wives. When she brought in a good corn crop, she ended having some extra cash on hand she decided to have a big blast to celebrate my fifth birthday. It turned out to be a success with lots of food to eat and music provided by a marimba band.

For my part, I tried to follow up anything that came up that provided interest. I and the timekeepers' two children decided to go visit the Ulua River, a very wonderful body of water 150 miles long in great Sula Valley. When we got there, we found that it was quite shallow. So we started walking on its bottom. We went about a third of the width across its considerable width then we became afraid since the depth had reached up to our shoulders and were afraid that we would fall eventually into an unseen depression since the river was muddy, and you couldn't see the bottom. After our effort we were exhausted. I was told that at a distance was a whirlpool. I was interested but not enough to go the distance to find it.

Despite the lyrics to the march of our pompous dictator that bragged about his building bridges and constructing highways when you reached El Progreso you found that there was no bridge to reach the other bank. It was necessary to cross the river to catch the train on the other side that would take us to La Lima and thence pay a fee to ride in private cars used as taxis to take travelers down the dusty highway to San Pedro Sula, the commercial center of Honduras. In order to cross the river a wooden barge with a leading cable had been set up, and it was powered by poling it. Unfortunately, the cable had a tendency to break and the barge would take off down the river. Before it got too far the boatmen would pole it back to the desired spot on the other river bank. Mom would enjoy this boat trip since there were vendors selling thick pork rinds and yucca. The starchy yucca tubers when boiled are like potatoes. My mother would take the trip to San Pedro Sula to visit old time friends she knew before she became isolated upon marrying my father and retiring to the plantation. She definitely wanted to catch up with what was happening in civilization just as my Father went to this city to get hardware supplies.

Life at our plantation home was done without electricity. There was a wood stove on whose embers you could roast beef on a skewer. The smell of the meat was really enticing. Butter was churned in a hand churn from the fat gathered from the top of milk bottles. Ice cream could also be made by turning an ice cream churn surrounded by rock salt. Both the butter churn and the ice cream churn operated on human labor, and it seemed like it took forever to get results.

To supplement the food we could produce locally we became acquainted with American with useful household items. For example, we could get at the Company commissary Calumet baking powder, Carnation canned milk, Lifebuoy soap, Lava soap, Dutch cleanser, and such. Since the name of the Colgate toothpaste means in Spanish, "hang on," lewd wits would make a phrase using its name to say, "colgate de mis huevos" that would translate, "hang from my balls."

The only food items other than the canned milk were mainly prunes, raisins, dates, and pickled olives. This list demonstrates that no fresh produce was available. So, once again you had to fall back to eating bananas or plantains where available.

Chapter Ten
Joyful Life

Wasn't it wonderful for you and me to have been little kids free from the worries of life? The main beings in my life were my two parents. Where on earth could I have found two more loving beings? I was their sole child at the planation home and therefore I had complete monopoly of their love. And, of course, I had the animals from the wild to provide me with joy and attention as well as the domestic ones.

The most outstanding was my medium sized black male dog, Coal. He was such a sweet animal full of unconditional love. He had an English name since the English language was in common usage in our family and from the very beginning I was conversant in both Spanish and English. These were my first important steps that would eventually take me one day to the United States and citizenship.

My father had learned his native German when he was born in Berlin. Besides, he also had to pick up Switzer Deutch, the Swiss dialect, and along the way he snatched up French, learned English when he lived in Texas which proved essential to be a planation manager and get along with the American bosses of the Company. And, of course, he needed Spanish in order to communicate with his plantation employees. So, at the plantation home I would speak English with my father and my sister when she came home from the boarding school in El Progreso and Spanish to my mother, who never learned English, and to her son, my brother Andrew.

I loved when my brothers and sister came home. During her summer vacation, my sister and I would sit under a tree and she would read out loud to me from a Spanish translation, a beautiful gilt-edged edition full of lovely engravings of the *"" on that*. It was an heirloom my grandmother had left us. Other than them, the other human companionship were the servants and the head plantation workers who spoke Spanish. These men taught me to curse like all get out. They also had fun with me.

One day one of them asked me, "What do you use your pee pee for?"

I answered, "To pee."

"That's all you use it for?"

"Just to pee."

They would burst out laughing.

In my innocence I had no idea in which other manner a penis could be used.

The plantation workers would talk a great deal about many things like the types of rifles such as those of the policemen including the Company law enforcement people who carried Mauser rifles of different models. I became aware of many subjects from listening to them.

I really didn't have many conversations with my father. He preferred to be by himself enjoying his hobbies such as improving the sound of his radio by getting larger speakers and fashioning out of mahogany the speaker boxes with his hand tools which he kept in a huge chest of drawers. He only had hand tools since electricity was unavailable except when he listened to his classical music at night. So, I loved to watch him soldering and doing other mechanical things such as cleaning the electrical generator whose valves needed maintenance from time to time He also would type letters to my sister and my brothers wherever they might be. While I didn't carry on conversations with Dad, I did bombard him with all sorts of questions. It was wonderful that I had an old father who treasured having me in his aged years and would be extremely patient with me. He pretty much could answer all of my questions. When I was born, he was already old and had a lot of worldly experience. I often would ride behind his saddle when he went inspecting the plantation in the early morning since the tropical heat of the day would rise pretty fast. He would putter around the house in the afternoon and take a nap. Then after listening to his classical music at night he would turn in around nine o'clock. He would awake around four at night, turn on the kerosene lamp that hung by his bedside and read for a while before going back to sleep.

I was learning more and more songs sung in Spanish since my mother loved to sing, and we also had a crank operated Victrola to play 78 rpm records. My mother had a beautiful voice, and she and I would form a duet. A couple of the songs were real tear jerkers, and we would sing and shed tears together. One mentioned the love of a young lady who was called "the daughter of the penitentiary" since her father was the warden.

The song related that she never had felt love, she only knew of the suffering of the convicts. But one day she fell in love with a prisoner, and that made matters very difficult.

My mother ran the household through the cook and a servant girl who washed clothes by hand in a wash tub. She also raised money growing corn to support my brother Andy's stay in the boarding school in British Honduras as Belize was called the 1940s even though she was not supposed to be doing so on Company land. She also fed field workers rice and beans and tortillas even though, again, the Company big shots might frown at the practice. She really had no choice since my dad's salary did not amount to much with the ceiling pegged at one hundred sixty-five a month since the Company gave him so many benefits.

He was stuck and had to go along with whatever the Company paid him. He was elderly man and in Honduras his chance of finding other work were nil.

Many years later when I went to see my brother, Georges, or who we called simply "George" in 1976 in Switzerland he told me that our father had inquired about the possibility of going back. But my brother told him that he was much too old and would only be a candidate for welfare. Therefore, he had to stay in Honduras for better or for worse. Such are the narrowing range of choices, we have to make, and they are increasingly limited as we grow older and older.

At the age of seven it was time for me to go to the city of San Pedro Sula to begin my education and that of my sister Betty and my brother Andy for them to go to high school. Now my mother and father had to face financing our education.

Chapter Eleven
Enjoying San Pedro

Nobody in San Pedro Sula called the city by its full name. San Pedro sufficed. My mother had chosen a house in an area, a barrio, called "El Benque." The house had many bedrooms. It had a small porch. It mainly served as a lookout as to who was walking up and down the street and to watch out for vendors with pushcarts that came along selling scraped ice snowballs. I especially like the little horse cookies from a nearby bakery made from bran flour.

Speaking of food brings up a point. On the farm with its limitations, food variety was minimal. Part of the education that I gained in the city was getting acquainted with Honduran food preparations. Honduras has delicious native food. My mother prepared delicious, generous Honduran tamales wrapped in banana leaves and boiled. Montucas also employ corn but while its kernels are still soft. These are cooked in corn husks. With corn or flour tortilla wraps you can include all sort of items as in the case of baleadas. wraps made with the pulp of plantains are particularly scrumptious. Honduran hard cheese finds its way into many dishes such as quesadillas.

Stews are a great part of Honduran diet especially the tapado that uses dried beef quite like jerky cooked in coconut milk broth. Another is called mondongo that includes diced tripe, that is beef or pork stomachs.

These foods bring up the fact that I was taught to eat the whole animal. Beef tongue is a delicacy. But other parts of the body also had their place such as brains cooked with scrambled eggs.

Coloring adds temptation with saffron rice and the red of the achiote. You also had to take into account the native plants such as the nuts called coyoles that come in a particularly hard coverings. They can be cooked in molasses. Orchata is a drink made from rice or jicaro seeds.

Tropical fruits grow aplenty in Honduras to satisfy any taste. Although I was also familiar with imported fruits such as apples, pears, and grapes, there were also native guavas, sapotes, caraos, guanabanas, and cashew apples. And, of course, tropical fruits familiar in the States such as mangoes, pineapples, and papayas. Even on the beaches you can find beach grapes and icacos. Breadfruit can be a substitute for tortillas or plantains. I also enjoyed freshly squeezed sugar cane juice.

Street vendors sold prepared foods, and in the mercado you could find among the market stalls small kitchens preparing native foods at very low prices. I detested vegetables, but Mom was so very happy that I liked V8 juice that made its content appetizing especially when sweetened with white or brown sugar.

San Pedro had in our vicinity other characteristics besides foods that enticed my curiosity. The small front yard of our home had as its distinctive oddity that someone had abandoned a store sized steel safe on it. I wondered if there was something in the safe. But no one ever bothered himself to open it and find out what mysteries it might contain. I never asked my mother to have someone mess with it since as a kid my mind went from one subject to another without dwelling too much on anything. It's a virtue that us as adults should have retained, especially those of us that tend to fret about one thing after another and agonize about what the future might bring.

A barber and his family lived in the barbershop across the street. They were talented musicians that with two guitars and a mandolin kept up with the latest Latin songs and could be heard practicing when no customers appeared, to the delight of me and my mother since we were great music lovers but unfortunately had no talent for playing musical instruments ourselves.

Even though we could not play, we did love to sing. My mother loved a Mexican waltz by the name of "Alejandra." The song described the beauty of the lady and told of how a fellow adored her from the first moment he saw her. The melody of the waltz is right up there with the quality of the much more famous "Over the Waves." My mother practiced and practiced singing the tune. My father said that she had a beautiful voice, and it was a shame that her talent had no outlet. Opera singers have to be able to sing in various languages and my mother despite the fact that English was spoken in our family never went beyond learning but a little of it. Be that as it may, my mother continued to practice the song. The only local radio station at the time had an amateur hour. To add to the fun of the activity, the disk jockey would-be lying-in wait for the singer to screw up the lyrics at which time he would ring the bell, and sadistic humans would gloat at the downfall of the poor singer. My mother did not give it a try.

Since our home occupied a corner of the street. The next corner across the street directly over by the barbershop was a small grocery store. I would make a few pennies by returning glass bottles of soft drinks to the shopkeeper. Behind our home was an abandoned bakery. My mother got the idea that she might rent it. She wrote to someone in New Orleans that at one time had been her stepfather and got a recipe book from him. With the help of my brother Andrew as translator, she managed to make marshmallows. They were put up for sale in a coffee shop downtown. I can't remember that the production of the treat was ever a success.

I haven't mentioned the name of the street on which we lived. The main street of El Benque sufficed. And the street address was nonexistent. If someone mailed a letter to my mother, it was enough to mention her name. The post office delivered the mail on a name basis.

The street in front of our house, as well as all the other streets of San Pedro including the ones in the business district were unpaved.

The fact that the street in front of our house was made of dirt containing stones was important. The boys in own neighborhood developed a sport of cursing each other at a distance and then tossing stones at each other. But we kept it at a safe distance. So, we could raise hell with our stone throwing and curse hurling and just put up a bold front. We would make up new curses.

Down a few blocks down was a medical clinic. It was the main place to get medical care. And about two more blocks further was the Cuartelito, that is "Little Fort," that was like a police station with the policemen wearing khaki uniforms with long sleeve shirts, pith helmets, and carrying Mauser rifles. They were considered poor trash and possible more of a danger to the community rather than a help.

My mother had to establish a complete home for us when we arrived in San Pedro for an education. This was so since back at the banana plantation almost everything in the home belonged to the Company. The Evangelical Mission School headed by the American Auler family was chosen for me and my sister. We would climb up the street to reach it. San Pedro is surrounded by mountains in the Sula valley, and the elevation in the city goes up it approaches them. I suppose we had to hike about a mile to get to school. While my sister,

Betty, was completing her education to become a Normal School teacher, I was studying in the elementary school that taught a class in English reading and spelling. We had to pay tuition at the school. It couldn't have been all that much. The missionaries also had students from really poor families. If the kids turned up dirty, they were stuck in the showers to clean them up. The message was, "You may not help being poor, but that doesn't mean you have to be dirty."

I enjoyed being a student at the Evangelical School. I particularly enjoyed being a student in the wood shop. My mother would laugh when I would refer to my instructor as "the wooden teacher." I made a small shelf to hold books. Our teacher explained to my mother that it was large enough since people had few books.

Happily, then San Pedro was a safe city with local festivities to attend. Besides the dances at the Municipal Palace at the main square of the city, there were other activities going on. Included in these was the election of a festival queen. The choice was made by how much the wealthy people of the city were willing to pay at the auction to have a particular candidate become the winner.

There were other festivals. Included one in which little kiddies rode on floats dressed as angels decked out in white with attached wings. I wanted to be one of those darlings. But I was promised that the next year I would participate. That, of course, never happened. The scarcity of money in our family and now the additional expenses of renting a home in the city, paying for our educations, and so forth had to be a factor. When my father came to town, I would go downtown with him since he would spend with us a few days. He mainly would shop at the Larach hardware store. It was owned by a fellow of Lebanese descent. All Middle-eastern people were called "Turks." The name came about when these Arabs first appeared in Honduras at the end of the Nineteenth Century their homeland was under the domination of the Turkish Ottoman Empire. So they carried Turkish passports. They and the Chinese controlled commerce in Honduras. The Chinese had grocery stores and manufactured fireworks. I remember them being bags of the fulminating powder with a wick attached and with a thin bamboo strip as its support stick and tail. The Chinese were made fun because they could not say the r sound. People would sing to them the mocking song which went, "Chinito, Chinito toca la malaca, Chinito." That would translate as Little Chinaman, play the maraca, a musical instrument and all they could say was "malaca." Both the so-called Turks and the Chinese were considered foreigners and somewhat despised for their financial success and were considered unassimilated and envied for their desire to help their kind get ahead.

The local native merchants weren't as successful. The predominant viewpoint current among the native Honduran population was that the native businessmen too often were interested in making just enough money to have food to eat the next day and had no need to stress themselves to strive mightily to get ahead.

In every case, the commerce and wealth were made possible in great part by the United Fruit Company's banana activities that brought money into the country.

Actually, the so-called "Turks" got more and more involved in local activities and tried to participate in the community. The extremely popular Honduran song "El Bananero" was written by a lady of Lebanese descent by the name of Lidia Handal. It tells about a fellow from a banana farm with the outlandish name of "Guaruma Dos" bringing to market his "green gold," and proud of being a banana producer. The Lebanese and other Arabs including Palestinians and so forth were originally or became Christians.

My father, like others from foreign lands working for the Company, were "gringos" and also held in contempt by the native Hondurans as additional undesirable exploiters of the country. He did not obscure the fact that he was not a native by the telling the peasant workers, "C'mon, quick, quick." And so, they used his words as a nickname for him.

Chapter Twelve
Our New Life

My father's token salary was found wanting more than ever to cover the cost of educating my brother, my sister, and me.

Once again, my mother was faced with providing an education for all three of us and needing to generate funds on her own. So, with the extra bedrooms of our home she started a boarding house with food and shelter for us as well as others.

My sister and I enjoyed going to the Mission Evangelical School. She at the high school level call it the Normal School level, since she was to be training to be a teacher with two years of preparation.

Andrew went to a school to learn accounting. I had never been to school at all since I was just seven years old.

The Mission Evangelical School was a Protestant institution. It was run by Lutherans from the Eastern United States. An elderly American lady named Mrs. Schiedt and her son Arnold ran it. Another elderly lady played the piano, and we sang hymns praising Jesus and his precious legacy. Most of the hymns were translations into Spanish of hymns such as "Tell Me the Story of Jesus" or "At Calvary." There was another hymn that spoke to our hearts regarding the full armor of a Christian with 1) the belt of truth, 2) the breastplate of righteousness, 3) the shoes of peace, 4) the shield of faith, 5) the helmet of salvation, and the 6) sword of spirit. Since from being a child I was fascinated by things of a military nature, I clearly remember this hymn.

The lady at the piano also composed a hymn of her own that said that school with Christ in it was such a happy place.

I was completely amazed to be surrounded by so many children since at the plantation I was mainly used to dealing with adults and a no more than a couple of children at a time. These belonged to the timekeeper and lived by us.

So, I was shy and tended to be by myself at first. The teachers and school administrators were amazed at my excellent behavior and were getting ready to give me a prize for such an exemplary student. However, as the saying goes that the devil never sleeps, one of the neighboring kids whom I had considered my friend told the administrators that they were barking up the wrong tree. He revealed to them that at home I was a hellion with a nasty cursing vocabulary to go right along with it. I had learned to talk with curse words for emphasis and liberally sprinkling my language with them such as was the vernacular of the peasants that I had made my own. What a friend this kid turned out to be! As the saying goes, "With friends like this."

I really had a loose mouth. I continued to be raised loosely. My parents' way of raising me was to let me go my way, and I would discover on my own how to behave.

I certainly was given free rein to express my views. Someone called this type of a raising a child, "to bloom in slack."

One day when my mother and I were passing the cemetery where my maternal grandmother was buried I asked my mother about her death.

"Where has my grandmother gone, Mamma?"

"The precious angels have taken her to Heaven."

"You tell those sons-of-bitches angels to return my grandmother."

I could be an embarrassment when I was around.

Once, when our front neighbor's retarded son died and was lying in his coffin in the parlor of the house I noticed that the corpse had teeth showing. This was a great opportunity to launch into a stinging, unrestrained observation, "He died like a dog showing his teeth."

When we had a party at home, and someone popped a bottle of champagne and consequently, the bubbly came spurting out, I remarked: "That was just like Macario's pecker shooting off!" Obviously, I had watched Macario, a house servant, playing with himself and the resulting eruption from his male organ.

My sister was growing up. In fact, at the plantation I had pointed out: "Betty is putting out tits." My sister was such a pretty young lady. This led suitors to seek her attention.

One of such gentlemen placed in his hand a biplane I had constructed from the hollow branches of a papaya tree. While he was fondling my airplane, one of the wings came apart. I wasn't going to condone such an intemperate behavior. So, I shouted: "Son-of-a-bitch put the plane back together!"

My sister was also liable to make unintentional faux pas because of her limited command of Spanish since she spoke English with my father just like he did with me and she spoke English while she had been attending the boarding school run by American teachers in El Progreso town. Once at a funeral she told the grieving widow in Spanish, "I congratulate you at the death of your husband." Fortunately, my mother stepped in to correct the situation.

I got together with kids in the neighborhood and threw rocks at the other boys down the unpaved street. As often happens when kids or adults go wild, accidents are bound to happen. With the devils of ourselves not holding back, a stone landed on the glass of a little girl who was sitting on the steps of her house drinking water. The glass shattered, and her poor mother let out a scream when the blood started oozing out.

Boy! Were the neighboring kids a wild bunch!

My mother was a very tolerant with my behavior. Perhaps much too much!

A young lady stayed as a boarder in my mother's home. She like to take showers in our shower stall. One day I decided I would stand on a chair and take a peek at the fine body of this pretty young darling since bathroom walls in Honduras came about a foot short of near the ceiling. She detected me admiring her in her total loveliness and let out a shout about my action. She moved out and my mother lost a live-in tenant.

My mother and I were very close. We would sit together and sing tear-jerking tangoes as we had while living at the banana plantation and tears would fall down our faces as we sang. One of the songs told of a man running off with a woman and neglecting his mother who was left not having any food!

My mother at one time had a young man whose family lived on a lovely banana plantation home situated on a bluff by the Ulua River. He definitely was the black sheep of this family who originated in Scandinavia. Not aware of this, Mom let him stay with us. One day my mother caught him with his knees pinning down my arms as he was preparing to cover my face with a pillow. Mom got rid of him right away. This one of the several times in my life when I could have died.

On another occasion my poor mother used the drawer of a pedal-powered Singer sewing machine to keep her cash. The lock was a very simple one and didn't take a master safecracker to open it. The same troublemaker that tried to murder me passed by the house and my mother saw him going down the sidewalk away from our home. My mother was struck with the premonition that something bad had happened.

Sure enough, she looked into the drawer of the sewing machine where she had placed the monthly money my father had sent her to help take care of our upkeep. Since the miscreant had lived with, us he knew when the money would come in and where my mother would store the funds. He nimbly stepped in, stole the money, and kept on walking calmly down the street.

The needy money gone, my mother broke down and cried like I had never seen her before and the tragedy broke my heart. I would have given anything to have had the tears that fell from her eyes turned into diamonds.

Chapter Thirteen
The Joys of Two Worlds

The delightful memories of the plantation with the largely carefree life full of the liberty were now past. I looked forward to enjoying them once more when the two month vacation from the San Pedro Sula Spanish school arrived. But having come into civilization definitely had its advantages. The kilowatts were flowing out of the electrical receptacles without interruption day and night. No longer were we subject on depending on the plantation's home generator's limited operating time of just a few hours per night with my father generally monopolizing the time with his classical music. I enjoy classical music but these were the swinging times of the big bands. It was time for the hep cats to get together with both Spanish and English lyrics. And since we young folks were bilingual we could delve in both worlds. Truly this was a golden age of popular music with hit after hit being produced in all of the Americas. Now we could listen right along with my mother to radio stations such as HRP1 and later HRQ that introduced the modern tunes. The Latin compositions were of such great quality that soon United States folks were enjoying imports such as the music of "Green Eyes" and "Perfidia" among others that the swing big bands adopted. And Xavier Cugat with this Latin music band became a big headliner in places like the Aragon Ballroom and was included in many movies.

We were enjoying hearing unlimited music from the radio as well as the live music we listened to from the musicians from the barbershop directly across the street.

They would come along and serenade us when one of my sister Betty's suitors went on a chaperoned date including my mother—and I wasn't about to be left behind.

We enjoyed the charming songs of the musicians at the banks of the Chamelecon River with its rhythmic waters near San Pedro Sula. My sister Betty's date was a charming fellow who owned a fleet of automobiles since running a car dealership was his business. Mincho was his name and he loved to say in Spanish, "Become an eagle, eaglet!"

Mother and I enjoyed visiting the HRQ local radio station where we could watch the deejay spinning the platters with the 78 rpm records on them. We admired the announcers' gift of gab and since they were local celebrities it was a treat talking to them when they were off the air. And there was dancing at the municipal hall of San Pedro Sula. Even though I was just a kid I insisted on going with my mother and her friends to the dances. And I definitely could be persuasive.

Coming back full of joy one night we heard a coughing sound coming from under street. The men approached the sound and found out that a child had accidently lost a fifty-cent piece that had rolled down into the street gutter. He went into it to retrieve the coin and was trapped underground. Good thing that the men of our party rescued him before a pouring rain drowned him.

Even though my family lived moderately well, I couldn't help but notice the poverty of Honduras, a third-world country with enduring wretchedness. Even when we would ride the trains of the United Fruit Company one could help but notice as we passed by the wild cane and mud huts with their thatched roofs of the subsistence farmers. As a little kid I asked my mother if people lived in such a dwelling. It made me appreciate even more the standard of living that the Company allowed us to enjoy although it was just a transitory one.

I still remember when I started school the delight of receiving my first book.

It was just a thin reading book with a flexible cover with a rubber feel to it. It had a delightful new book smell to it and reminded me of the odor of a brand-new linoleum.

The classes at the elementary school of the Evangelical Mission School were conducted in Spanish. My sister went to the Normal School high school level to prepare to be a teacher, and I went to the elementary one. Mine was called a Preparatory School.

The local wags made fun of the name of my school level and said it was "the preparing the donkeys level." The three years I spent there I was able to learn to read and write the Spanish language. In addition, I fortunately had also a class to learn to read and spell the English language.

I especially liked recess when the boys would get together to play soccer. We played it in a very strange way. A hundred students might be on the field all at the same time. Out of that number about twenty would line up at the goal, and all twenty would be goalies. The remaining huge crowd of opponents would do the best to kick the ball through the goal. Talk about a lot of madness of kicking going on as the ball violently shot back and forth. Competition on a playing field is one thing. But to have a real battle going on is completely different.

Another activity the kids engaged in was to drop a gob on chewing gum down the hole in the ground where there was a tarantula burrow. The hairy spider would grab hold off the sticky substance, get stuck, and readily be pulled up and out. I really didn't appreciate the capture of the creature. My being around all sorts of living beings at the plantation led me to appreciate the value of life and the right to existence and respect.

When I first started school, I sometimes would walk home all by myself when I would pee occasionally into my short pants on the long trek home. I remember young ladies looking at me in sorrow and pitying the poor little kid--me that is. When the elementary school would let out around two o'clock my mother wanted me to take a nap. After I would lie down, she would ask me if I was awake. I would answer, "Yes." I finally caught on that I was being stupid. One day when a lady visitor happened to be with her, she asked me if I was napping. I did not answer so my mother said, "I think he did go to sleep this time." Of course, I was only pretending.

At night the kids of the neighborhood would gather by the streetlights and play question and answer games and hide and go seek. I found out that hiding under the chicken wire covering of a garden plot was superb-- I had found the perfect hiding place under which no one could ever find me.

Like any school child I could hardly wait for the two-month vacations to arrive.

I could go back to the plantation and be like the lord of the land. And the Company did make facilities available to spend time away from the usual plantation routines. One summer my mother and I went to the beach at Puerto Cortes at a Company beach hotel called "Campo Rojo" meaning Red Camp. We enjoyed the surf and sand and eating steaks and red snapper to our hearts' content. We were loving the relaxed atmosphere. Running up the tab was of no concern in "our live life for the day" state of mind. We ran up a goodly tab while we ate like kings and listened to the "Peanut Vendor" song sung in Spanish that was so popular in those days. Whenever I hear that evocative melody and its charming lyrics, I am back at such a lovely stay.

My father with his small salary and his penny pinching practically blew a fuse when he found out the amount of the bill. But it was well worth the expense since it was a vacation I have never forgot.

Chapter Fourteen
Rising Spirit

The beautiful, sweet hymns we sang at the Evangelical Mission School out of a little blue hymnal praising Christ were a blessing with which to start the school day. I went with my sister to church. of the Evangelical Mission and to Sunday School. I appreciated the Christmas cards sent by our fellow Christians of the United States. I especially liked the colored metal foil that some of them had. Even this small token of fellowship highlighted the greater world Christian community. A Catholic priest would come to stay with us at our plantation home. He amazed me in that all he would eat would be bread and honey. He gave me a comic book with illustrated stories of the lives of the saints. I remember one about a saintly lady who when she put on gloves her hands burst into flames. This happened because she had yielded to vanity.

I didn't get any religious instruction from my parents.

My mother was Roman Catholic but did not put much of any effort in it. My father I found out considered himself an atheist. Coming as he was from Berlin, Germany, at the end of the Nineteenth Century when the likes of Schopenhauer and Nietzsche with the "God is dead" frame of mind were all the rage, he was carried along with this way of thinking. He would point out as outrageous Jesus' words at the cross when he cried out that God had forsaken him. The memory of the First World War when the so-called Christian nations butchered each other's populations didn't help.

My maternal grandmother, Emma, from what I was told by my family members on my mother's side, was a proponent of the Virgin of Suyapa, the patron Roman Catholic saint of Honduras. She put on a great celebration to honor her.

The festival was held at her home, and she went all out to make the event a memorable one. My Aunt Vida continued her mother's tradition. My mother although as not as active a Catholic as members of her family had been, remained Catholic until her dying day. In fact she was buried holding a rosary in her hands.

As far as politics was concerned my mother felt herself to be a member of the Liberal Party and made no effort to hide the fact. Honduras was ruled by the Nationalist party with the country's dictator, General Tiburcio Carías Andino as its leader, My father was fine with the dictator since it meant stability for the Company. Having a strongman as president meant holding down labor unrest but was harmful to a country going forward as far as the democratic process was concerned. In 1944, a demonstration against the dictator appeared before the large fort within the city of San Pedro Sula. Machine guns opened fire and killed many demonstrators. Despite the lyrics of dictator General Carías' march that claimed that he was constructing bridges and building highways one had only to take a look around and wonder about that. The pathetic, leaky wooden barge used to connect El Progreso to the other bank of the mighty Ulua River was revealing of how much a bridge was needed. The streets of San Pedro Sula, the industrial as well as the commercial center of Honduras had dirt streets. Instead of having them paved they were occasionally torn up and then a road grader would flatten the dirt all over again. The road from La Lima and San Pedro Sula was also unpaved. The cars traveling it raised enormous clouds of dust.

It was said that Carías promoted air travel. Certainly, the DC3s connected the cities of Honduras. This move certainly did not excuse the pitiful state of the road networks.

Another thing I learned at the Evangelical Mission was to be patriotic. This meant learning the national hymn of Honduras whose name translated as "Your Flag." It has a lovely melody, as do some of the other patriotic hymns such as the one dedicated to the pine trees with their precious greenery. The fifteenth of September, the national Independence Day holiday, we would find all the kiddies dressed completely in white and marching along. The celebration made me feel that Honduras was a country to be proud of. It was always pointed out that the country's main hero, General Francisco Morazán did his best to unite the five Central American countries into one federation after their independence from Spain. He even went to war to try to achieve this. But ultimately the five nations decided each to go their own way.

It's interesting to note that you would think that these five countries would be very similar. But they can be quite different. For example, Honduras is highly westernized, and you would never find a pure-blooded Indians wearing native outfits.

But in Guatemala, right next door, you see Indians dressed in their pretty hand-woven costumes made with looms at their homes. They're colorful and truly works of art.

Even the passing of many years you still have feelings for a country where one was born, spent your youth, and whose tropical beauty you enjoyed.

In San Pedro Sula the Central Park still exists and so does the kiosk in its middle.

Facing it is the city hall, known as the Municipal Palace, where dances for various events and organizations were held. And on the opposite side of the park is the relatively new Catholic Cathedral. To the left side of the Municipal Palace, modern times are exemplified by a new hotel where the high concrete walls of the burned-out fort stood for ages.

My mother and I would enjoy a walk around the the park when the weather favored it. I have an indelible souvenir of such a stroll. One evening when a festival was being held in the park, I was walking along when I observed two dogs having sex. I came to a sudden stop when my head crashed into one of the park's cast iron light posts.

The blow opened a wound in my forehead whose scar still remains.

I'm glad that the old buildings of San Pedro Sula still remain. But the ones constructed by the Tela Railroad Company, the subsidiary of the United Fruit Company, in Tela Nueva that I held dear have been smashed away including the ones that made a difference in our lives such as the hospital where I was born. Still memories of those days gone by recur, such as standing in the Mess Hall, also now destroyed, and inhaling the pungent smell of buttered toast mingled with whiskey fumes which were perfume to my nose as the sea breeze wafted through its screened walls.

Here I am dressed in white, the prescribed uniform to wear for the Honduran Independence Day celebrated on September 15th. It's the same date for other Central American countries with Mexico's being the next day.

The schoolchildren all dressed in white would be gathered at one end of San Pedro Sula's Morazan Avenue, and we would march up its length. An Army officer would try his best to form us up to march into formation. At one Independence Day celebration, he would command us to open fists and then close fists. It was as close as he dared to have us follow military orders!

The one delight in the whole affair was the ascent of a hot air balloon that we followed with thrilled eyes as it ascended into the sky. Fortunate for me, the three times I participated in the parade, we had clear, sunshiny days.

The Independence Day observation highlighted Honduras' famed historical leaders.

Honduras, as well as the rest of the rest of the Central American nations, achieved their independence from Spain in 1821. The editor of the Declaration of Independence was Jose Cecilio del Valle from Honduras. General Francisco Morazan from Honduras desired that the Central American nations remain as one country. Morazan was federal president from 1830-1834 and 1835-1839. But social and political forces were too strong to maintain the union, and they separated into the five republics of Central America.

For the first three years I attended grade school in Spanish and this period allow me to learn something of the country in which I lived besides just the American culture of the Company.

All these are beautiful memories of the Honduras of long ago. They remind me of the poem of Sir Walter Scott entitled "The Lay of the Last Minstrel:"

Breathes there a man with soul so dead
When never to himself has said,
This is my own, my native land!

Chapter Fifteen
Moving On

What motivated my mother to leave my home in Barrio El Benque?

She did not consult with me. And she in her headstrong way of operating would do whatever the will-o-wisp path her flighty character led her to take. Never mind what others thought. As she succinctly put it, "Children are governed by their parents." Our move took us to an adobe house down the main street of San Pedro Sula and placed us next door to Diario Comercial, the main newspaper of the city. But now I wonder what would an adobe house be doing in the city? Was it one of the original dwellings in some ranch on the outskirts of a town that grew up to be a city and now was within its boundaries? Good thing it had a good roof, or our home would have melted away from all the rains of a tropical climate.

I sorely missed the kids I had known while we lived in El Benque. I no longer had them to play marbles or spin tops during the day. And at night we had enjoyed playing hide

The Lay of the Last Minstrel and go seek as well as sitting in a circle playing word substitution games such as the one about a ragged soldier that was missing his rifle, pistol, and so forth.

El Benque was well located since it was near the center of the city where most of the daily outstanding events took place. The most dramatic was the burning of the huge fort on the side of the municipal park. As the flames enveloped the structure, you could actually see the flames from my house. An alarmed citizen cried out as he passed by, "The fort is on fire and they're taking out bombs are the fire spreads and if they would blow up it would be a horrendous disaster!" I guess the city's fire truck with its boiler in the middle looking more like a tea kettle on wheels was not up to incendiary powers of the blaze.

Since my family no longer lived at El Benque, I had to explore the possibilities of our new surroundings. I soon found out that the home across from us belonged to a family of foreign origin. They were something other than natives of the United States. In those days my knowledge of geography was very limited. That family had a son about my age of eight years old. He had a lot of toys. I didn't have much of anything. In fact, playing with the kids out in the street seemed to have been mY greatest form of entertainment when I lived at El Benque. Once in a while the mother would give me a toy out of the warehouse of her kid.

And next door lived some “Turks” with a grownup daughter of about my brother Andrew's age who was then in his late teens.

One day I discovered on our yard across from the young woman's house a bunch of items that looked a lot like balloons. I picked one up and examined it. It seemed strange that the item had such a wide area to blow on. From overhearing my mother speaking to another adult, I pieced together that the items in question had something to do with sex. At the time sex was an area I hadn't given any thoughts out of my carefree kid days. But my mother one day approached the young “Turk” woman and asked her, “Andrew looks kind of worn out these days.” Without hesitation the shapely lass grabbed her crotch and said, “I suppose he's been getting too much of this.” The location of their trysts must have been in the storage building in the back of the property where the gal lived.

Anyhow, I developed an interest in the newspaper next door. It especially gained my interest since one of Mom's boarders was into doing drawings in India ink, and one of the reporters got interested in my sister Betty.

He was the one that my father called “Green Eyes?” Just like the name of the song.

This fellow loved to wear sunglasses, thus the nickname my parent gave him.

Mincho Paredes, the fellow with all the cars was still dating my sister but now that we no longer lived in El Benque with the barbershop musicians across the street, there were no more serenades at the banks of the Chamelecón River. He still seemed to be the best candidate for my sister's hand. I loved the fact that the cars on which he took us on drives around the city were always the latest models. One day while he was driving, I turned the ignition key off and the vehicle stopped. Ole Mincho wondered if something had gone wrong with the battery. But I rapidly told him what I had done out of curiosity.

I grabbed at anything that made life interesting to me. I could hardly wait when the man with the pushcart and the block of ice would shave it and add syrup to make a snowball treat for me. I improved on it by adding condensed milk. As a kid I didn't worry about calories.

I liked the fact that we lived close to the Avenue of the Lions. I enjoyed the statues of the lions. The civic leaders of San Pedro Sula had given thought to having these avenues here and there in the city just like they took pride in the main square of the town with its municipal palace in front of a park that had in its center a large band kiosk.

But of the sites of San Pedro I enjoyed most of all its city market, "El Mercado" with all sorts of things for sale. I loved the crafts that poor people made to earn a little money Some created tin trucks and other such toys out of discarded tin cans. They also provided us with the tops we used to spin as kids. I particularly liked the actions toys. I remember there was a clown made of thin strips of wood that when you squeezed the sticks near its legs they would make it do a back flip.

Also, at this time my parents became members of the Lions Club, the international society with charitable inclinations. Years later when we no longer lived in San Pedro Sula, she proudly would mention to people that she had been a member of the Lions Club. She was a very social person, and you could tell that she was glad to be away from the isolation of the banana plantation. No doubt she was able to reignite some of the social relationships she once had when she'd lived in the city with her mother and sister. Her sister now lived in Puerto Cortés just about a couple hours travel on the railroad. You had to switch trains at a place called Baracoa and get off the Company train and get on a train of the National Railroad when we lived on the banana plantation. But living now in San Pedro where the National Railroad originated you could get on it and go all the way to the port.

My mother was not through moving while I did the last of my three years in the mission school. We next moved to a house on an outlying area of the city. Sometimes my brother Andrew would carry me on the handlebar of his bike. We would pass a convent from where emanated the overwhelmingly delicious smells of pastry items being baked. My brother was an interesting fellow. He smoked a pipe with Half and Half tobacco in it. And he loved taking out a .45 automatic pistol and playing with it as he cleaned it, worked its slide, and snapped its trigger mechanism. His interest in firearms may have been stimulated by the fact that his family on his father side had a military history. His father,

Raoul Matute, did not have an interest in the armed forces since he was busy running his car repair shop in San Pedro. But his grandfather definitely did. He was General Andrés Matute, who bore the same first name as my brother. Grandfather Matute actively participated in the revolutions of Honduras' turbulent times around the beginning of the Twentieth Century. He was an officer. A song tells that he was ambushed on the bridge of the town of Choloma. The ditty goes on to tell that this Matute was promoted after this incident since he was shot in the butt. Andy's interest in firearms got him in trouble. During a train trip the police searched the passenger's luggage for weapons. They found a pistol in one of my brother's suitcases. He was taken into custody, and his father had to get him out of jail. The search for firearms on the train was justified. Passengers sometimes got into gun fights especially if they saw an enemy on the train including members of a family who were subjects for a series of avengement incidents.

Andy would mingle with middle-class young people and often wear a suit. He would always leave our home wearing a fedora hat.

My brother was also into various firearms since he was a hunter. My father, by contrast, had no such interest. While inspecting the plantation, he would carry a .22 pistol as a sidearm. This was the only firearm he possessed in addition to a one-shot shotgun. My father, while I was growing up, did not have a dangerous confrontation with peasants. They, of course, constantly carried razor-sharp machetes that could lope off a human head with one blow. I was told that, before I was born, my father was involved in a shootout. For some reason, unbeknownst to me, a group of men decided that they would attack the plantation home where my father lived. After the shooting was over, one of the attackers was left dead while the rest withdrew. Neither my father nor the men who helped defend the farmhouse were charged since it was held by the authorities to be self-defense. With one exception. One of the men took his machete and struck the dead body some slashing strokes. He was charged with desecrating the dead man's body.

My father had a temper that he would express at some of the peasants even calling them "damned whoremongers." There were people at the farm who would gladly find a way to get back at him. Once he brought back a pineapple, after a trip to El Progreso. We ate the pineapple and my mother saved the rinds. She then proceeded to soak them in sugar water in order to make a mild alcoholic beverage through the fermentation of the rinds. Someone went to the authorities to snitch that my father was producing illegal alcohol by making the slightly alcoholic chicha. My father was picked up by the police for being a bootlegger and only released after he paid a fine.

There was no doubt friction between employees who were native born Hondurans and the gringos, which would include my father. A vivid example of a deadly confrontation took place when a disgruntled Honduran entered a meeting where he had a grudge with an American. The Honduran fired a pistol at the American who was sitting down, and when he stood up, received additional shots in his body. The shooter was imprisoned as a murderer. But in some quarters, he was hailed as a hero as demonstrating that a gringo better not push a Honduran to a breaking point through disrespect.

I was glad that my brother Andy did not get into plantation affairs. He was definitely a city fellow. My brother was a complementary male figure in my growing concept of what a man could be and act. I also was grateful for his saving my life. The banana plantation where we lived had concrete lined irrigation canals carrying clear, swift water. To our way of thinking it was the closest thing to immersing our bodies since bathtubs were unknown in Honduras and certainly we did not have private swimming pools.

So, one day my family went, and we stuck our legs into one of these irrigation canals. Unfortunately, I got too adventurous and fell into the rushing water. But, fortunately, my brother Andy snatched me to safety out of the water where I would have stood a good chance of drowning.

When the irrigation canals were shut off at the closure point a pool of water was left. A few minnows were trapped. My father took one of them and put them in a bowl for me and picked some pond scum to feed it. But things did not turn out as expected. The little fish stood still in the water while a long string of feces hung from is body. Any trouble it had did not last long. The minnow disappeared. No doubt one of our cats decided to make a meal of it.

The fact that my family was close to the Americans living in Honduras and greatly under the influence of the United Fruit Company made me and my siblings English speakers. Thus, it was logical that while we lived in San Pedro Sula we would have contacts with Americans living there.

My brother Andy got to know people at the American consulate. Thus, he was able to bring a movie projector from the consulate to our home to watch movies. It did not matter that the movies were of the educational type. As a kid I really enjoyed the ones with cartoon characters. But to have movies at home was something totally unexpected in our Honduran home.

My sister and my mother formed an interesting pair. They would gather together at a person's home when someone would come back from the United States on a Company ship with things she had bought for resale in Honduras. The ladies would compare notes as to what the latest American fashions were at the moment. This included outfits featuring the red, white, and blue American colors as befitted a country that had just won World War Two. Honduras was an ally of the United States and has continued to be in the many wars that America has been a belligerent.

Once in a while someone would enter our family's life who was interesting. For example, there was a man who had a hand that had been grazed by the bullet fired from a Mauser rifle of one of the trashy policemen. Someone who lived with us treated the wound by running a restorative fluid over it. I could not determine if the police were still after the man. From what I could figure out he was not a criminal. But he was a wanted man for his political beliefs.

At the time, if you stayed out of politics you could prosper. My brother Andy became known as a fine amateur soccer player and was called “Caserini.” Hondurans loved soccer and one player, “Coneja” José Cardona got to play in Spain with the Atlético Madrid.

Chapter Sixteen
Involvement of Many Kinds

My mother would take me to a malt shop in San Pedro Sula that she would run into other ladies she knew or where she could make new acquaintances. She would also be able to take notice of how other women dressed and find out what was the latest in town since the newspaper did not have a social column. One day, at said tasty establishment, a young gal appeared with tap dancing shoes. I wasn't aware of such a novelty. True, there had been Hollywood movies that came to Honduras usually about a year after they had been shown in the States. They were in English with Spanish subtitles. This was a great arrangement since if you were bilingual and had a hard time following the dialogue when someone appeared with a strange American accent that was hard to follow, the subtitles covered for this deficiency. I wasn't the type to follow after movies involving fancy dancing and a whole lot of mushy romance. I was inclined to the ones that had a whole lot of action and would bear as well as I could the pestering scenes of lovey-dovey kissing and the like. So I wasn't acquainted with tap dancing or any other terpsichorean activity. Well, the gal with the tap-dancing shoes tried to put on a demonstration of tap dancing in the malt shop. It became obvious, even to me with my ignorance on the subject, that she was no great threat to outshine others engaged in this type of dancing.

But what the heck, it was a free demonstration and something new. She was giving rousing applause anyhow for displaying the novelty. Anything that was American was admired and the trends and fads were keenly observed.

My mother liked to travel and visit people who she knew in different places. She was acquainted with a Martinez family in El Progreso. The Martinez family was interested in social activities and were well in tune with the social events and gatherings of the interesting people of the United Fruit Company. These family members were attractive and socially adept who would easily fit into any social gathering. I was fascinated with women. I admired whatever my mother and my sister did to make themselves devastatingly pretty.

When we visited the Martinez home, I watched how one of them styled her hair by increasing its volume by inserting rats in it. These rats, despite their name associated with nasty critters were rolls of hair that were placed on the head and covered with the living hair. The men of the house were also a source of admiration. I watched them how they butchered a hog at home. They would introduce a long knife under the hog's head that would sever a heart artery and lead to the animal's death. As it bled, the stream of blood was gathered in a pan to make it into blood sausage. I then would watch how the hog was butchered and sliced up into various cuts of meat. Skin with the fat attached was chopped into pieces and then fried to create pork rinds and the resulting lard would in part be saved or mixed with soda ash and turned into rough soap.

As always, I was averse to water touching my skin. So at the Martinez home I entered a typical shower stall—one of those whose walls had a foot of wall missing at the top. Time went by and it was obvious big time that I was stalling and continued to do so indefinitely. This was just a tempting situation so one of the Martinez gals took a pan of water and poured in on me after reaching over the wall of the shower stall. Hell has no fury like a kid who has been treacherously assaulted by a stream of cold water. I shouted at the female perpetrator of this heinous assault all sorts of fancy forms of cursing I had learned from the other kiddies.

Both my mother and the Martinez female gang must have laughed until it hurt at both the treacherous act and my subsequent rage. I could hear my dear, loving mother, the prime source of my trust, shouting, "This is killing me!" Followed by additional gales of laughter from the other female perpetrators.

The Martinez, as an outstanding family, was held in high esteem by the El Progreso population. The beauty of its women led them to be crowned queens of festivals. You could see them all decked out in fanciful costumes covered with sequins and rhinestones and draped with sumptuous robes, a high regal collar, and a lengthy train, the very picture of the female royalty like those appearing at Mardi Gras balls in New Orleans. Being socially prominent was one thing, meddling in politics quite another. Mr. Martinez became outstanding opposing the dictatorship of that elite that backed the conservative crowd intent of exploiting the country to their hearts' content. He was playing with fire.

I have no doubt that he knew it. But as a man of courage and high principles he could not hold back expressing his outrage at the criminal and illegal actions of the powerful. His actions infuriated the corrupt. Thus, it was just a matter of time before they retaliated. So, Mr. Martinez was bound up, a rope tied at his ankles and dragged to his death as his body was pulled down the streets by enemy horsemen. Poor Mrs. Martinez went into deep grief and sorrow and so were we at the thought of the death of Mr. Martinez and the horrible way he was killed. Of course, the criminals were never brought to justice. My family was greatly shocked and deeply grieved that such a noble family would be assaulted by such a tragic, horrendous event of unforgivable brutality.

Chapter Seventeen
A Sea of Changes

My sister finished her preparation to become a teacher. And my brother, Andrew, got himself a job as a toolmaker. He must have obtained his position through the influence of my father. He worked in a Company railroad shop. There was a need to keep the wheels and the shafts of the locomotives and the rail cars turning smoothly. His job was to place the equipment on a lathe and redefine its turning ability. He became so proficient at his skill that he never lacked a job either in Honduras or later when he lived in the United States. He was following in the mechanical footsteps of his father, Raoul, who owned a car repair shop in San Pedro Sula.

My brother, Harry, who had left home early own after my father married my mother, managed to build up his accounting knowledge and end up working for the accounting department in Tela for the Company and eventually worked with IBM equipment.

In the meantime, my father had stopped running a banana plantation. He now was the overseer of an abaca plantation. The abaca plant is a banana type plant with the leaf sheaths also forming a stem. However, it's not grown for fruit but for its fine fiber. It has been called Manila hemp. The abaca production in Honduras was under a contract from the United States government of the Reconstruction Finance Corporation with the United Fruit Company. A document from the US Department of State states that "Loss of Far Eastern sources of supply would make the United States almost completely dependent on Central America to supplement our strategic stockpile." The Reconstruction Finance Corporation helped the war effort for the United States during the Second World War. So, the United Fruit Company had got involved in that effort and still had dealings into the 1950s even though the war was over. Since the abaca plant is native to the Philippine islands the plantations where it was cultivated in Honduras were named after islands of its country of origin. My father's new plantation was called Mindanao. It was surrounded by other abaca plantations named after islands of the Philippines: Cebu, Luzón, and the one that with the headquarters and facilities such as basic shopping items, a tailor, and a dentist was called Mindanao.

I got started into enjoying the overseer's plantation home where we now lived.

It was a two-story house. On the first floor was the office and next to it was a large open area that held the rope making equipment. There were men would take the soft but strong processed fibers of the abaca plant and as they walked holding under their left arms a bundle of them, they would proceed back while twirling the threads into a rope. On the second floor were the living quarters with four bedrooms and the kitchen. My father occupied the screen covered bedroom facing the living quarters of the laborers separated by about a quarter mile of open area. On it grew an enormous ceiba tree. There was at the front of the second story a wide hall with sturdy wooden rocking chairs facing large screened windows. When it rained canvas rolls were unrolled and let down to protect the inside. And in Honduras when the rainy season really got going, it would rain for days on end. Out of these windows you could gaze on flowering shrubs as well as a drive from the front of the plantation home to the railway that passed by it. This path was flanked on both sides by oil-bearing nuts of African palms. You could hear the sounds of orioles that nested in them.

One night I descended the exterior stairway that led down to this area. I looked down the path and observed a glowing ball approaching. It glowed but did not give out light to the its outside like a lamp, and it moved straight ahead about eight feet in the air without moving up and down as a flashlight when carried by someone walking. I could feel something unearthly about it. I went back up the external stairway not interested in having it come right up to where I was standing. I have never been able to figure out a scientific explanation for this phenomenon. There is something called ball lightning. But while it glows just the same as the balled light I observed, it has the characteristic of jumping up and down as it moves along, not like the glowing object I saw that moved straight just as if it had been traveling along a wire.

In the back yard there was a large open space where the mules and horses were tethered. In it was also stored for safety the gasoline drum whose fuel my father used to run the electric generator so that he could hear his radio at night. At one time when I was standing in this open area, I felt something pass between my shoes and saw that a small snake had slithered through. I stood still as it erected itself and looked towards me. After a moment it lowered itself down and continued. It is said that the venom of a small, young snake is more powerful than that of an adult one. Behind the back yard was a wild area. It contained tea grass from which we could make tea. Once while I and my sister Betty, who had come to visit the plantation, were walking along the path at this location we heard the rustling sound of a snake. We ran away scared and we could hear the snake scurrying away in the opposite direction probably at least as scared as we were. To one side of the open area there was a small shed building. Although I had seen many shootouts on the movie screens while living in Sam Pedro Sula I had never fired a gun. So my father took me out there and allowed me to fire his .22 caliber pistol. I fired in the direction of the door of the shed that was made of heavy planks. After each shot I fired there was a rustling sound in the bushes near the shed door. No doubt these were ricochets bouncing from the hard planks. I wondered why my father didn't take into account the possibility that one of the ricochets would head our way! Beyond the shed there was a ground depression that held an artesian well water pump operated by underground pressure. This was a greatly welcome source of water unlike the windmill-generated one we had at the banana plantations that you could not gauge its content and might stop flowing while you were soaped up while taking a shower.

At Mindanao there was a one room American school. Its teacher was the wife of the superintendent of the abaca plantations, Louise Swofford. She allowed me to switch from the third grade I had completed at the Spanish school and start my studies at the third grade in English. Thus, I was faced with the prospect of having to finish the third grade in English with only the second semester left. Good thing I had classes in English at the Spanish school. Even with that background it was quite a stretch to make such a major change. Psychologically I was devastated when I first reported to this tiny one-room schoolhouse. There were barely a dozen students in all.

It was situated above a bar and sandwich Company run establishment. The first day I sat outside on the stairs leading up to the classroom and cried my eyes out. Gone were my familiar school surroundings as well as anyone I knew. I really had to struggle to keep up with students who had been schooled all along exclusively in English. My teacher felt that I had made enough progress so that I could be expected to pass on to the fourth grade at her tiny school. I was so happy when I received the news.

My situation was unique in that I rode a mule to school. My mother left San Pedro Sula where we had lived and returned with me to the new plantation. My sister stayed in the city and taught elementary school subjects.

This new plantation incurred changes. My father had to give away his beehives since the abaca plant produced no fruit and no flowers that would go with the fruiting bananas. In regard to the abaca cultivation, my father was an innovator. He noticed that the outside casings were thrown away. He suggested that they be used to produce low-grade abaca fibers. Thus, what had been wasted was saved, and additional money was generated for the Company. I can't remember that my father was ever awarded anything for his shrewd thinking that made the Company extra money.

Once we had returned from city life to living in the city, the marriage of my father and mother was not the same anymore and they separated. It was also time for me to separate myself from my parents. The little one-room school only went to the fourth grade so that in order to continue my education, I had to go to a boarding school at El Progreso in the Company side of the town. My mother continued being highly protective.

She rented a house in El Progreso to be near me. She tried to help me in any way she could. When there was a Halloween party held at the boarding school at the Company clubhouse, she had made for me a Zorro costume but not just any kind of material it had to be watered silk. And again, silk when I needed a costume to appear as a Wise Man at the Christmas pageant. She appeared every once in a while, when we came outside of the Boarding School to play. This was an embarrassment for a big, growing boy like me who did not want to appear to my peers as a momma's baby. So, she decided to leave and go to Puerto Cortés and be with my brother who worked there in his job as a toolmaker for the Company.

Since my mother resided in Puerto Cortés, on Fridays when the school let out, I had to take two separate trains to reach her home in the late afternoon. At least the first train belonged to the Company, so I did not have to pay. But when I boarded the train at a railroad junction called Baracoa I did since it belonged to the Honduran National railroad.

I then spent Saturday with her in the home she shared with my brother Andrew. With loving kindness, he took care of our mother when she and my father separated. On Sunday, I took the Honduran National Railroad train back to where I transferred to a Company train. I then rode a mule to my father's plantation that I reached by noon. I then left the following morning on a rail motor car that picked me up as well as the rest of the children at other plantations to go back to the boarding school. To think that there are kids in this world that have never been on a train and I used to ride several trains every weekend while the school was in session. This traveling situation was a blessing for me. While the other kids from the boarding school went home on Fridays to their respective plantations and were stuck with whatever limited facilities they had being out in the boondocks, I was enjoying the life of a city by going to the movie shows, the local festivities, and whatever pleasures city life would provide me as a young lad.

The boarding school was definitely a unique place, starting with its location, by a golf course built on an abandoned cemetery. The graves were bulldozed over and the only remaining signs that the grounds had been those of a cemetery were a few two-level individual mausoleums. The bottom floor of the boarding school held the classrooms. The sleeping quarters were on its second floor. On one side of the top story of the long building was the sleeping area for the girl students and on the other for the boys. In the middle section lived the lady and the son who ran the living quarters and supervised all of our activities. Our boys' beds were in a long bay with beds along its sides. We slept in a building built over a cemetery, and we were superstitious. This scared one of the boys who was assigned to turn off the lights. He ran as if a ghost was after him and dove into his bed. For the same reason I kept my head covered in bed.

I enjoyed playing board games with the boys at night as well as swimming in the swimming pool of the golf course club house. And everyone at the boarding school ate at a mess hall that had cooks who prepared restaurant level food for us at lunch and supper. At breakfast I first became aware of Cheerios, Raising Bran, Grape Nuts, and the rest of the cereals common in the United States since at the plantation I only knew of Corn Flakes and Quaker Oats for oatmeal-- prized for the glassware that came in the boxes. I was first introduced to meals that I was unaware existed. I enjoyed the ox tail soup so much that I asked for a second helping. The rest of the meals were a blessing well as a curse. We had full course meals at lunch and supper starting with soup and ending with dessert. The food that came in between was hell for me since the lady in charge of us boarding school boarders insisted that we clean our plates. Disliking something on our plates and not wanting to eat it was not an option. She would stand over us and force us to eat everything. I have to admit that I learned to eat and actually enjoy some foods that I was unfamiliar with at the plantations where I had lived. While at the banana plantation I had all the fresh fruit I could ever eat, including the plantains grove that provided me with the equivalent of bread to go with my meals. Vegetables and other kinds of fruit were unknown since no one bothered to grow them. The outside world did provide us with nonperishables such as hard, dry cheese but that was the extent of it. If eating bananas did not do the trick as having the necessary intestinal vowel movements, the company commissary did have the dried prunes.

I had been a picky eater who drove my mother to distraction when living in the city by being skinny and not being much of an eater. In fact, she was so worried about my thin body, that she paid me a dime a day so I would eat and not die from self-inflicted starvation. At the boarding school I had to eat, especially since the food was practically shoved down my throat. It was a good experience in that I learned to eat food that were discoveries to me even though I almost would vomit at the taste of some of the foods. Particularly, some of the vegetables that I found nauseating. To this day I still hate some vegetables such as beets and turnips.

In addition to the healthy food served at the mess hall, it was made sure that we

received enough exercise. The vast cleared land of the former cemetery was used mainly used as a golf course, and we played soft ball on part of it during the school day as our schools' physical exercise.

An American boy and I were the least athletic of all the boys and girls. So the teachers gave us an edge towards our building up our self-confidence by being allowed to pick who would be the players on our opposing teams. Among the bats used to swat the balls, there was a really fat one who I would pick up often with the vain intent of striking the ball further than I usually did. So the players out in the field figured that they would have no trouble catching the balls I struck. But one day, I picked up a regular sized bat and really sent the ball flying way past second base. Surprisingly, the next time I came up to bat I again sent the ball flying a long distance. But, alas, I was not able to duplicate this excellent performance ever again. Sometimes while we were out playing softball, men would show up playing golf. The fact that we had a ball game going didn't bother them. However, I did end up with a bruise one day when struck on the arm by a golf ball.

Again, the fact that there were still a few mansions of the dead still standing on the back and the side of the boarding school did not deter us from walking at night as a group under the pale moonlight with the evening breeze caressing us as we went along.

Sometimes as we walked at night, we would meet a young couple who we found out had been engaged a long time but never had taken the plunge to get married.

We were fortunate that we could enjoy the golf clubhouse where we could buy treats from its little store. We also enjoyed the Olympic-sized swimming pool where I learned how to swim. Diving was a different story. I would jump feet first from the high diving board.

At the close of day, we would take out showers and go to bed. Many a night instead of going straight to sleep with our young memories helping us when we would take turns describing a movie that we had seen.

Or telling lies. Told by the fellows that owned air rifles. They would brag that they would take them and pump them up fifty or even a hundred times so that the blast coming out of the barrel would be ever so devastating when hunting.

Never having an air rifle and not knowing how one worked, I was fooled by the lies since an air rifle does not allow for the ever-enlarging accumulation of air in its mechanism.

Behind our boarding school straight ahead across the golf course was the part of El Progreso that was populated by the local people. The immediate part facing us was a cluster of whore houses. When the passenger train would pass, you could see the women hanging out of the windows exposing themselves by wearing their bras. And through the open doors there were laboring types such as you would see working in the plantations whooping it up and dancing with the women in a most aggressive manner.

At night we could hear the jukebox music coming from these houses of ill repute. They would play Texmex corridos which are ballads spiked up by aggressive accordions playing polka style. One of the favorite corridos was "The Young Man Prisoner." Why this corrido was such a common choice was a mystery. It had heart throbbing music as well as heartbreaking lyrics about having to visit the miserable inmate. And the music would continue forever as long as there were farm laborers willing to spend their hard-earned money on the jukebox, on liquor, and carnal pleasures.

While there was sex at the distance, there was also was receiving sex education from the boys at the boarding school. My male classmates instructed me that my penis was part of the baby making procedure babies were not brought in by storks. With a woman as a sexual partner, it would be a divine experience. A penis could also provide free pleasure. My father would come to visit me at the school from time to time, and we would meet at the golf clubhouse. He asked me if I liked mambo music which was the rage in the early fifties. I said, "Yes." And he looked displeased. As so often has happened in history a new rhythm or dance is at first considered lewd and indecent.

Chapter Eighteen
On the Road Some More

My life led me to move around and see new sights. I was used to changing locations even while we lived in San Pedro Sula since my mother moved several times to new homes in different sites within the city. My father had also moved from one plantation assignment to another as the had chosen him to be its overseer. As a result of my parents' moves I had already been a student in several schools. So that traveling with my parents during our summer school vacations did not concern me by adjusting from one environment to another.

My father took me on a road trip to visit Comayagua, Honduras original capital, full of colonial buildings and its lovely cathedral that includes beautiful paintings of saintly scenes. Then we traveled to Tegucigalpa to look at the capital of Honduras and to admire the monuments built to beautify it. Of note were the Peace Monument beautifully situated on a hill as a reminder that Honduras' dictator had brought peace to the country after so many political upheavals including lots of armed insurrections. There was also the equestrian statue of Francisco Morazán statue dedicated to Honduras' native son who tried to keep Central America as one country. The pre-Columbian era was not forgotten. There was a park with reproductions of the wonderful steles and other sculptures found at Copán, Honduras' wonderful Mayan city with its unique pyramids such as the one with hieroglyphic staircase and other unique creations. The past was also recalled with the city's cathedral and its religious art. Tegucigalpa's presidential palace has a pretty stone Victorian exterior with a promenade on its exterior that looks down into the Choluteca River separating it from its twin city across the river, Comayaguela. As protection it had American bazookas installed upon its ramparts. It was engaging to see that Tegucigalpa's streets were paved with brick-sized stone blocks sculpted by convict labor. My mother also enjoyed traveling and since she knew people everywhere in the northern part of Honduras, she also had friends at La Ceiba where the headquarters of the Standard Fruit Company were located in Honduras. This was the rival banana company to the United Fruit Company with its branch, the

Tela Railroad Company operating out of Tela. The Standard Fruit Company had been founded in 1899 by the New Orleans Vaccaro brothers. Now it's called Dole Food Company. The beach at La Ceiba is really beautiful. The only thing I didn't like was that as you stepped along the bottom of the sea near the shore it was uneven so that all of a sudden you found yourself falling in a hole.

What thrilled me more than anything was a most exciting sight for my young mind. One day while my mother and I were enjoying La Ceiba's ocean location, I saw a Pan American Clipper, a majestic passenger flying boat.

My father would also go off on his own to a place called Erandique by himself while his children were away. There he would mine for ore bearing opals. He would bring the raw stones and make them into jewelry after placing them in silver settings. While my father was in charge of the abaca plantation, my brother Harry offered me a chance to go with him to Guatemala City. I jumped at the opportunity.

We left Tela on the good United Fruit Company ship, Antigua. It was a refrigerator ship that hauled bananas, mail, and cargo as well as having cabins for passengers. Several sister ships were owned by the company, and I hoped that eventually I would add one of or more to my list of traveling vessels. The names of the Company ships came from places bordering the Caribbean Sea. The Antigua was named after the island of Antigua in the Leeward Islands. Dining onboard was first-class starting with the luxurious table settings with genuine silverware. And the menu had numerous delicacies to choose from.

Mealtimes were announced by a steward striding about while playing continuously a ding-dong series of notes on a small glockenspiel. There was entertainment aboard ship including a costume contest. One lovely young lady turned up in a dress exclusively created by attaching together telegram sheets of paper. Naturally, she won first prize.

When we got to the Guatemalan port of Puerto Barrios, we rode a railroad through difficult mountainous terrain. We crossed a bridge that that ran over a tremendous chasm with a terrifying look down from a dizzying height. When we arrived at Guatemala City, the capital of the Central American country of Guatemala, we thought we had missed supper since we arrived at our hotel around eight o'clock at night. Wrong! We were arriving just when the meal was about to be served.

Heck, the movie theatres started their showings around eleven in the evening. In Honduras we would have been long asleep. We were used to the American way of running our schedule of daily activities. We proceeded to visit Antigua, Guatemala. Zikes! That name sure reminded us of the name the ship we had just left. The place was indeed antique. Back in 1717, 1751, and 1776 it was struck by one earthquake after another. After having to rebuild time and again, the government gave up on the city and moved the government to the present location of Guatemala City. According to our guide, one of the nearby volcanoes also added a tsunami when its crater exploded, and it released a torrent of water that ran downhill and into the already devastated city. A goodly part of the city was left in ruins in addition to the remarkable colonial buildings that were rebuilt. The whole of it making for a romantic setting. To add a note of spice, our guide mentioned that there had to be some illicit hanky-panky among the supposedly celibate priests and nuns since skeletons of fetus were found by explorers among the ruins.

Harry and I also traveled to Lake Atitlán and cruised around. The name in Nahuatl means “at the water.” It certainly is a beautiful lake and is surrounded by majestic mountain peaks. We really enjoyed being in the interior of the country and visiting native Indian markets and observing the beautiful hand-woven textiles including the garments worn by the native people. Since Honduras is the only Central American country without active volcanoes it was quite a sight for us to see a mountain spewing smoke in Guatemala. In some areas of thermal heat, you only had to stick a water pipe in the smoldering earth to get hot water. But someone made a joke by saying it all was fine as long as the volcano did not decide to enter the home through the pipe. Since we were staying in Guatemala City, we were interested in walking about and looking at the sights. The main square is dominated by the huge five story presidential palace. Nowadays it is called the National Palace of Culture. It is a huge building constructed in a combination of Spanish baroque and Spanish renaissance styles covering 8,860 meters. It was built during the years 1939-1943 of the dictatorship of General Jorge Ubico.

The outside is of a greenish color made by mixing concrete with oxidized copper so as not to have to be repainted over and over. Its color allows it to be called “The Big Guacamole.” Green was the

Here you see me astride my mule, Timburiaco, "Fat Bellied," that used to take me from my father's abaca plantation, Mindanao, to the one-room schoolhouse at the headquarters location that was like a small town on the local Company headquarters, Bataan. Since the product of the abaca plant was Manila hemp, the plantations producing it were named after Philippine Islands. The rest of the abaca plantations were consequently named Luzon and Cebu.

My mule was lucky in taking me to the one-room schoolhouse. Some of its kind had to carry the abaca trunks on their weary backs.

My mother at one time owned two horses, a sorrel (reddish-tan coat) and a salt and pepper or "steel" gray.

I can't recall much of anything as to the gray horse, but the sorrel was another matter. I remember it as a huge horse. I rode it at the about the same age as you see me pictured, in my early teens. I would pull on the reins to try to slow it down. But it completely ignored my efforts. It decided it had a mind of its own.

My mother entered it at the racetrack of La Lima, a city in Honduras that was mainly another Company town.

I decided to bet on our own horse. Not a problem. It was raced over and over the same day on the small track. I won money every time.

This photograph shows in the background the large house the Company provided my father as the plantation overseer.

This is a photo of my little niece, Leslie, the daughter of my brother, Harry, and his wife, Blanca.

Leslie is holding a bouquet made out of flowers gathered is the justly famous beach of Tela, where travelers from all over Honduras gather during the Holy Week vacations.

In the background you can see the out in the sea dock jutting into the bay that made Tela an international port for the United Fruit Company, or as it was called in Honduras, the Tela Railroad Company.

It was beautiful at night to stand on this structure and hear the waves rushing through its supports while feeling the delicious sea breeze soothing your whole body, especially when the moon would shine on the surf.

Fishermen with harpoons would stand on the deck of the dock and try to get a night's catch.

Many nights and days the conveyor belts standing on the dock offloaded banana stems from railroad cars into the holds of refrigerated banana ships.

Unfortunately, this in-the-ocean dock no longer exists. An all-consuming fire destroyed it especially since the supports and crossties were made of petroleum creosoted wood.

Now only a stump near the shore is all that remains of it. One of the main features of the port of Tela is just a memory right along with the outstanding buildings of the Company that were eventually torn down with the passage of time as the Company moved its headquarters to La Lima.

Here you see my brother, Harry, and me at Lake Atitlan. This body of water is formed by the immense bowl of a volcanic crater.

In contrast with Honduras with no active volcanoes, Guatemala has many. It's something to get up in the morning and see a volcano spewing smoke.

Harry and I on this particular excursion also visited Antigua, Guatemala, a small city with colonial buildings many of which were destroyed by volcanic action in 1773. It was exciting and spooky to visit under one of these destroyed structures.

According to our guide, Antigua, Guatemala, was shaken to pieces by the shaly eruption of the Volcan de Fuego, "Fire Volcano." To add to this catastrophe, it was also ravaged by the Volcan de Agua, "Water Volcano." This latter one let go with the water it had stored in is crater and sent a tidal wave into the city.

We went by bus to Lake Atitlan while staying in Guatemala City not far away. We had landed at Puerto Barrios, the main port of the Central American country of Guatemala. We sailed there on the United Fruit Company ship, Jamaica. While it still was a banana vessel, it also had cabins for passengers. The food was plentiful and delicious. And we even enjoyed a costume party. Best of all since both my father and this brother were employees of the Company, we could travel for free.

After we landed at Puerto Barrios, we traveled by train to Guatemala City. We crossed at one spot on a bridge that stretched over a very deep chasm. That was really scary.

dictator's wife favorite color. The dictator had traffic lights installed in the in halls of the building! If the red lights were on, it meant that the dictator was walking through the halls and nobody should get in his way. If the lights were yellow, the government functionaries could walk about. And if the lights were green, anyone could move throughout the building including the janitors.

The inside is also outstanding with staircases that have elaborate brass balusters. They are a treasure in themselves. They can be rotated so that they can be easily polished on all four sides. The most majestic area is its grand salon. It has a chandelier of Austrian crystal weighing two tons, and there is a report in circulation that an employee is hired for the sole job of keeping it dusted. There is another large reception hall with a chandelier made of solid gold. The interior features beautiful murals depicting the history of Guatemala. And we could not help but notice that here and there on the façade were bullet holes that meant that the massive structure that does look like a fancy fortress with towering sections at each end of the façade had its share of the country's internal turmoil.

Guatemala City struck me as a progressive city with many interesting shops. I was delighted to see that it had stores with lots of toys I had never known anywhere else.

I made sure that I bought several tin soldiers as well as an artillery piece that had a spring that slammed out lead cannon shells. This was a toy that I had never seen in Honduras.

We left Guatemala on a twin engine DC3. Good thing that the pilot was a smart fellow. He began racing the plane down the runway and then decided that it was overloaded. So, he returned it back and had it lightened before we flew back to Honduras.

Chapter Nineteen
Education in Many Ways

One evening while we were having supper at the dining room where we had our meals at the Progreso American School as a boarding student, I received a telephone call from my father. He informed me that my sister Betty had gotten married in New Orleans. That created quite a stir among my fellow students and a cry went up of congratulations. My sister had looked forward to having a really happy marriage, and she even had filled a hope chest with items that she felt would delight a child. I thought that it was a wonderful event. Hearing of a wedding is akin to hearing the news that someone had found a buried chest. Everyone is full of hope. Perhaps it's filled with treasure!

Since after the sixth grade I had reached the limit of the academic offerings of the Progreso American School, we in the family decided I would continue my education in New Orleans while staying with my sister who had always looked after me just like a second mother. I had really enjoyed walking with her to school while we both were attending the Evangelical Missionary School in San Pedro School. We would walk home from our classes to eat lunch at home. Then when we heard the march "Hands Across the Sea," we would start back.

When my sister finished her courses to become a normal school teacher she began to exercise her profession. Before she left for New Orleans, she had been teaching the children of rich Americans in San Pedro Sula. They begged her to stay and even offered to raise her salary. That was understandable since my sister had always been a sweet, patient person.

My brother, Harry, his wife Blanca, and I were going to travel to see my sister on the Chiriqui, another United Fruit Company ship of the Great White Fleet. It was named for a Panamanian province on the western coast of the country. Panama was one of the many countries where the Company had extended its empire. It is interesting to note that the Chiriqui like some other of the Company's ships served the United States war effort during the Second World War. It was renamed the USS Tarazed (AF-13). It was 447 feet long, with a beam of 60 feet, draft of 26 feet, and displacement of 11,880 tons. It could travel at 18 knots which is like 21 miles an hour propelled by turbo-electric powered engine with twin screws. During the war it bristled with many antiaircraft and antisubmarine guns of various types and calibers. It served the US Navy in the North Atlantic, the invasion of North Africa, and supported the invasion of Southern France. It received a battle star for its service. It was returned to the United Fruit Company through the War Shipping Administration at New Orleans. In civilian use it could carry 95 passengers. When we boarded the Chiriqui bound for New Orleans we weren't aware of its heroic history and how the Company helped with its ships the war effort. I did remember when I traveled with my father to Puerto Cortes as a child during seeing a banana ship with a gun tub at its stern with what looked like a twin Bofors 40mm guns while the Second World War raged.

I was so happy to have arrived in America on a student visa. I was glad to see my sister Betty again since she had been like a second mother as I grew up. The fact that the home of the in-laws where my sister had a television set that in 1952 was still a rarity was a truly welcome item.

I loved going to the movies, and television was then in its "Golden Age" with comedic stars such as Milton Berle, Cid Caesar, Red Skelton, and Jimmy Durante. There were boxing matches and fake wrestling to watch on one hand and on the other cultural shows which even featured famous opera divas singing in most cases popular tunes.

At this period in its history television programming was at least trying to have a cultural side to it and trying to avoid being called the television set "The Idiot Box" or the

"Boob Tube" since it featured a well-endowed blond with low-cut dresses called Dagmar.

To me any television program was enjoyable and didn't matter to me that it was called "The Great Wasteland." Some students while I was at the Progreso American School came back talking about the Huey P. Long bridge, which in those underdeveloped days was the salient feature of the city. Now I felt that I had finally arrived in the United States, which to us in the American schools we had heard so much about and was the Promised Land. Besides television there was the jukebox of Funk and Manny bar just a few yards away. I enjoyed its music sung my greats such as Kay Starr, Patti Page, Perry Como and Hank Williams. They were also featured on the television Hit Parade.

While in New Orleans, I attended Sophie B. Wright Jr. High School on Napoleon Avenue. I particularly enjoyed the vocal music class where I became more aware of the songs of Stephen Foster and other old songs like "A Bicycle Built for Two," and some more lovely songs such as "Look for the Silver Lining." This music reminded me of my experiences in the American Schools of the United Fruit Company. We used to march up the stairs to the Bataan American School to the martial music of "Stars and Stripes Forever." At the Progreso American School I added old favorites like "I'll Take You Home Again Kathleen." And my favorite, "A Capital Ship."

My sisters-in-laws were poor people, but they were kind to me. On Sundays they would prepare a bone-in beef rib stew to die for. But it was apparent to me the poverty of the menu. Not necessarily the ingredients, but their lack of variety. The meats were the usual chicken, beef, and pork commonplace cuts. While I had grown up eating pretty much all the flesh of the animals and enjoying dishes such as scrambled eggs with brains and dishes such as mondongo containing tripes. These folks would not have gone far afield with dishes using tropical ingredients such as the coconut broth of a tapado that included sun-dried beef and ripe plantains. It all made me wonder if the Americans living in Honduras were any different. Did they enjoy the wondrous Hispanic Culture the way we loved that of the United States? Particularly the music of the Big Band Era?

Or did they stay with what was in the pages of the Saturday Evening Post? But their children seemed to be more inclusive with them taking to dancing La Raspa.

I stayed in New Orleans for my seventh grade and then returned back to Honduras on the Antigua. I really loved the city and wanted to return to live in it. The only negative side to my stay in New Orleans was to find out that my sister's husband was a charming, lazy drunkard that had no intention of leaving the shotgun house where he sponged off his retired parents. Unfortunately, my kind, sweet sister was as unaware and misled. She thought that men in the United States were all like Clark Gable and Gregory Peck. I looked forward to the day when I could restore my wonderful, sweet sister to a level of prosperity she enjoyed when living with my mother, even though she was the stepmother to my sister. But the poverty-level life was behind me now. Now I could regale in the luxurious amenities aboard ship such as the excellent dining with heavy, real silverware. It was also great fun to be on the Company ship and enjoy the company of other teen-age students of my age returning home to Honduras. My bunkmate turned out to be a fellow in love with his switchblade knife that at the time were not illegal. I sure hoped that he wouldn't get rabidly angry and stick it into someone certainly not me. The kids enjoyed playing the shipboard piano with tunes still current at the time such as "Heart and Soul" and "Blue Moon." Someone had the bright idea that I play the piano. That was a definitely an inaccurate assessment. True, I had taken piano lessons while I boarded at the Company's Progreso American School, but after my father came by and noticed the pathetic progress I was making, he cancelled further instruction. I wasn't turning into a child prodigy like Mozart.

As an additional treat, the Antigua laid anchor in Havana, Cuba's harbor. Back in 1953 Fulgencio Batista was still the dictator in charge.

I was able to get off the ship and tour on foot the Malecón of Havana. It's a combination of a wide scenic esplanade and seawall. I also took the tour of the Morro Castle that had guarded the Havana in colonial times and the Spanish defenders even had laid a chain across the harbor to keep enemy vessels from entering. I clambered all over the fortifications and even peered over the battlements to have a splendid view of the ocean and the seacoast. I had to be careful not to get too close to the edge and endanger myself by falling off and crashing onto the boulders below. I enjoyed admiring the cannons from colonial times as well as the installation of modern artillery. The castle had also been modernized by the addition of a lighthouse. Inside the castle was a gruesome tableau. It showed a man mannequin sitting down and with blood pouring out of his mouth and nose and even his ears as he was slowly strangulated by a garroting machine.

The guide of the castle tour relished pointing out just how brutal the Spanish could be in colonial times.

The Morro Castle reminded me of the Omoa Castle a short distance from Puerto Cortés in Honduras. It was the largest Spanish fortress in Central America. There you were able to see rows of cannons and piles of cannon balls as well as the hollow ones that were filled with gunpowder in order to have them explode like the modern artillery shells.

The Omoa Castle was built to store the silver coming from the mines that used to be around Tegucigalpa, whose name means "Silver Hills" in native Indian language. The richness of the place allowed it to take over being the capital of Honduras from Comayagua. It was off the coast of the Omoa Castle that Jean Lafitte, the same one who helped Andrew Jackson win the Battle of New Orleans by supplying him with flints for his guns and destroying the British advances with artillery accuracy, where he lost his life. Jean Lafitte after being pardoned by Andrew Jackson moved his base of operations from Barataria, Louisiana, to Galveston, Texas. Lafitte saw two galleons leaving from Omoa and hailed them to surrender. But the galleons instead set full sails and continued to light signals to each other Lafitte thought that these galleons would be lightly armed with just a few cannons and the crew armed with muskets. What he hadn't observed was that on the sides hidden from Lafitte's sight were rows of heavy cannon. So, Lafitte was in for a big surprise. One of the sailors of the galleons who was in the rigging shot and killed Lafitte. Lafitte's second of command was also killed. It was then that the pirates called off the fight and fled. Eventually the nations who had colonies, the English, French, Dutch, as well as the Spanish had it with the buccaneers, corsairs, pirates, and other "sea dogs" who began to attack them all without distinction, decided to get rid of them. It is interesting to note that Honduras was and continued to be a very rich country in gold and silver mines. At one time the Spanish rode on horses with gold horseshoes! Back in 1953 the question came up now that I had returned to Honduras whether I would go back to the States to continue my education. Since after working so many years of working for the Company, my father was now at the prescribed retirement age according to Company policy. He was about to retire and would no longer have all of the freebies that went with his job. With new expenses he would not be able to continue sending money to the States so that I could continue living there with my sister.

Therefore, it was decided that I would stay with my brother Harry and attend the Tela American School for the eighth grade. I loved my brother Harry and it would always be a delight when he would come visit us at the abaca plantation. We enjoyed going to see him in Tela. But it was a tiresome journey. We would have to keep changing trains all day and finally arrive at Tela in the early evening. We would spend just a few hours with Harry, and then go to bed to get ready to get back on trains to head back home. The visitor housing where we stayed while at Tela was of exceptional cleanliness and care associated with the Company's management. The hand-ironed fine linen sheets with which we covered ourselves was at the level of excellence typical of Company housing.

As soon as I started attending the eight-grade at the Tela American School I found out that my public-school learning in New Orleans at the junior high level was considerably backward in comparison with the advances at the Company school. I only knew about fractions in Math. and these kids were into percentage and decimals. And I knew next to nothing in grammar structure. My deficiencies were such that my teacher even suggested that I go back to the seventh grade. Once again, I was faced with the dilemma of having to play catch up in school. But I toughed it out and was able to graduate from the eighth grade.

While staying with my brother Harry I helped out by looking after my little niece, Leslie, five years old and her little brother, Allen two years old. I loved the beautiful beach at Tela and loved walking it with them. We acted like beachcombers after each of the gales.

I enjoyed my classmates at the American School. I was amazed when a fellow showed up to be with us from the Honduran Bay Island speaking English with an East Indian accent. I was curious at his unusual intonation. My graduation of the eighth grade showed the decline of my father's economic fortunes since my he couldn't afford to get me a suit for graduation. In Honduras you didn't buy suits off the racks. Each had to be individually tailored. I had to cobble together a borrowed sports coat and a pair of pants whose different shades of blue clearly indicated that I wasn't wearing a suit like the rest of my fellow students. My poor economic condition left me out of my fellow students' progress. They could continue their education in the States at New Orleans high schools like Holy Cross, and I didn't have the monetary means to do so.

So I hung around a couple of years just doing reading anything I could get my hands including a world history book whose content I almost memorized. It eventually helped me when I took the Western Civilization courses with famous Stephen Ambrose at LSUNO as UNO was then called.

Then when my brother Andrew emigrated to the United States and was in the Army, he started sending allotment money to my mother. I started taking correspondence from the American School located in Chicago in effort to restart my lost education. This led me to do well when I emigrated to the United States in 1958 and joined the U.S. Army and took its GED test and I scored in the 90s. When I was honorably discharged, I received a high school certificate from Warren Easton High School located on Canal Street in New Orleans.

I lived in my father's home in San Pedro Sula and my mother's in Puerto Cortés.

And I returned to Tela to stay with my brother Harry and look after mainly of his same two children once again. My little nephew Allen was an agile little rascal. He would playfully run away from me and did so cunningly by scurrying under the Company's raised homes. I had to run and crouch trying to catch him. But he, I, and his sister, Leslie, had good times together at Tela. We loved, as always walking the beach and doing beachcombing looking to see what the surf had brought in. A lucky fellow living in Tela, after a terrific storm, found on the shore a pair of Spanish cannons with admirable workmanship.

We weren't as fortunate. We found from time to time banana tree bottoms, which is where the banana plant lives, that were still good after having traveled on the sea. I planted them in the back yard of my brother Harry's Company provided house since he did IBM accounting for it. Unfortunately, at least once, a stray mule wandered through a neglected open backyard gate and would start munching on the banana leaves of the banana trees on which I had pinned my hopes.

In the meantime, I and the children took all that Tela and its beautiful surroundings had to offer. If civilization was wanted, you could walk the old iron bridge that led from Tela Nueva, the Company workers' side, to that of the Honduran native population. There you would find movie houses. Once I took my little niece, Leslie, to watch a horror movie called, "The House of Wax" starring Vincent Price that I had already seen at the Prytania on Napoleon Avenue in New Orleans. That night poor Leslie was unable to sleep. Her mother told me, "Never take her to another horror movie."

Another way to have fun was to window shop at the stores in the downtown of Tela Vieja. And you could also walk in the park. It featured a bust of the former dictator, Carías. On the pedestal someone had written, "I'm your daddy." There were also celebrations going on in Tela Vieja. One included the crowning of The Ugly King who nevertheless had the chosen most lovely young lady around as his majesty's bride.

The national celebrations were also enjoyable with little kids singing and dancing and marching. The whole business reminded when I was a young lad in San Pedro Sula. The fireworks at night were another joyful part of the celebration.

It was during this joyful time with my family in Tela that I got to experience something sad and ugly. There was a woman next door neighbor whose husband also worked for the Company. Her son was more fortunate than I and had left for the States to continue his education that I in my poor economic condition couldn't enjoy. But an incident with her came up that shows that even close to home there is truly evil lurking in the hearts of men and even women. Little Allen, my little nephew who I was taking care while staying with my brother Harry, fell down and broke his arm. I rushed him to the hospital to take care of him, and he got a cast around his arm, and I brought him home.

But there wasn't a happy ending to the situation. The woman next door told my brother Harry that I had taken Allen on his little red wagon on the railroad track that ran next to our home and he had fallen on a rail due to my negligence and stupidity. Fortunately, I did not suffer the consequences of the woman's lies. What on earth possessed the woman to lie and try to get me in trouble? Did it have anything to do with her fortunate son leaving for the States to continue his education, and I had to stay back? I certainly had nothing to do with her son being gone. Why do some people go out of their way to do evil? I enjoyed the beautiful offerings with which Mother Nature had contributed to the beauty of the country. But the humanity that lived in it had shown its dark side once more. My plantation adventures ended with the retirement of my father from the many years of being overseer. He bought land on the outside limits of San Pedro Sula in Barrio Las Palmas where he built his home and one-room rental apartments.

Chapter Twenty
Lands of Beauty and Danger

Leslie, Allen, and I loved best of all our trips and even picnics at the arboretum on the edge of Tela called Lancetilla. Far from the maddening crowd of Tela proper, Lancetilla was a garden of solace. Its luscious greenery tended to eliminate heavy thoughts anyone would have of their existence. While walking along, you could enter the bamboo covering that rose up like the nave of a cathedral. And the trees would rise up to allow us to enter their groves that appeared like green mansions. And sitting by the gurgling brook completed the whole feeling of serenity.

The beauty had a practical angle to it. Sam Zemurray was always a man who was upfront in his search for cures to the ailments that threatened to destroy his banana business. The Panama disease has decimated his plantations by attacking the roots of the banana plants and the Sigatoka tried to ruin him when it became destructive of the leaves. The diseases were able to eliminate completely the Gros Michel banana specie. With its extinction gone was a flavorful banana fruit that people who had tasted it sorely missed. So, at Lancetilla he had a place where he could bring in other varieties of bananas. Not only was he interested in the survival of bananas, but he was also on the lookout for discovering varieties of lumber that could be of commercial value.

Back in 1925 Dr. William Popenoe began setting up the Lancetilla Arboretum. It was named "Lancetilla" because there was an abundant shrub growing there with spiny lance shaped leaves. The botanist was accompanied by his wife, Dorothy. At Lancetilla , a pretty pink fruit was added called Blighia Sapida also known as achee. It was brought originally to the New World from West Africa by the famous Captain William Bligh of the HMS Bounty mutiny fame. This fruit is edible but to eat it safely you have to allow the fruit to open naturally on its own and let it be exposed to the sun. The flesh is poisonous until allowed to be exposed to the light. And its seeds remain poisonous.

Unfortunately, Dr. Dorothy Popenoe ate the fruit before it was fully mature, and she poisoned herself. Her tomb pleasantly caressed by the tropical breezes of the Lancetilla Arboretum is located there. This plant is not the only one that is poisonous in Central America. A most common plant is the Chichicaste Grandis plant, simply known as chichicaste. It has nice green leaves with a hairy covering. If touched by human flesh, there appears a very intense burning lesion. It is planted in hedgerows around property to provide an aggressive wall of protection.

There's great natural beauty in Central America. While I was going to my school in Bataan from my plantation of Mindanao, I would hit a patch of forest. I once ran into a small herd of peccaries comprised of half a dozen of the little, hairy pig-like animals with tiny tusks hanging out of their snouts. I was lucky that I passed close to them, but they didn't pay me any attention. In large groups their aggressiveness is reinforced and can attack humans. Their little tusks are able to do harm. Thank God I never was confronted by a jaguar or a puma.

But nature has to be left alone or one will suffer the consequences. Most snakes would rather slither away than have to defend themselves with humans. But someone going through the bush one might step on a fer-de-lance or what it was called in Honduras “barba amarilla”, that is, “yellow beard” because of the light coloring of its mouth. Since it is several feet long, it might not only bite you on the lower legs, but it could fling itself at you, sticking its fangs in your thigh. You need to hurry to a medical facility to have antivenom injected into you since its bite could be fatal. And there were also many other poisonous snakes such as the coral and the tamagas.

One day as I was coming home from my one-room schoolhouse at Bataan on my way to my plantation at Mindanao I spied a cloud looking object hanging from a leaf of an abaca plant.

With youthful lack of intelligence, I swatted at it. I turned out to be hundreds of ticks hanging together. The ticks spread all over my right arm, and I did my best to get rid of them. But as was to be expected I missed some. One ended where it would find lots of blood—you know where.

The ticks were ugly but there were other insects such as beetles with iridescent coverings, butterflies with transparent wings, and others with beautiful patterns on their bodies. Outstanding where the gigantic beetles with fearsome claw-clamps heads.

To see the large sources of danger was one thing but what about the invisible ones. I have to mention the worms in a land of poor sanitary conditions are transmitted by touch and even by dust containing eggs that would land on your tongue as you spoke. Some of these worms would rapidly reproduce in large numbers in your intestines, and a tape worm could be several feet in length. A quack doctor claimed there was a method to get rid of a tapeworm. This consisted in eating a lot of papaya. Then you would sit over a bowl of milk. The tapeworm would come out of your body. But you had to relax and not squeeze your anal sphincter, or it would break off and not come out to its full length. One of the horrible intestinal worms has three heads that can produce 10,000 eggs a day right there inside your sweet body. To get rid of them, you have to take a poison to kill them internally and then have to flush out the dead with a dose of castor oil or Epson salts. Castor oil has a horrible taste. I was advised it would be easier to swallow by adding orange juice to it. It still tasted awful and now you had to swallow even more liquid! Another evil was amoebic infestation which came through poor water. My mother had a stone filter through which water would flow but that didn't stop the amoebas from going right through and infecting one's bodies. You can see little children with huge bellies. These bellies are not so big because the children eat a lot. Most probably they are sickened with parasites.

Other sources of disease lurked everywhere including sick people who couldn't afford the medicines to get well. These would include those carrying tuberculosis who would spread the disease. I must have been infected by this terrible malady. Fortunately, I recovered from the illness. But I continued to test positive for having had a bout of it.

So much beauty in Central America but also so many dangers—to include *homo lupus*, man the wolf. I felt so embarrassed as a citizen of Honduras to have Mr. Harold, of the Evangelical Mission, an American to be present at a shootout at La Junta. These killings would take place to settle past accounts of some kind of business injury when two men would find each other riding together on a train or simply to settle a slight to one of the men's honor or as a response to disrespect. Just about two yards away on one of my train trips back to Tela sat a man with at least two .45 caliber bullets in his fat belly. Soon the train would be arriving and then the Company hospital surgeons would have to work on the weekend to save him from getting peritonitis and further endangering his life. A woman who was close to me chided me for being a youth traveling alone, "So, you see what happened? That's why you shouldn't be traveling without your parents." Would the presence of my parents have made any difference? Equally unexpected were actual shootings on trains that ended in deaths. The public in all of its wild speculations would raise "the hue and cry" of revenge. And many would wonder when the trail of blood would end.

Chapter Twenty-one
Volcanic Changes

Tela seemed as calm as ever. The traffic was minimal as it always was. Most people walked. People were used to doing so and the distances were not at all that great. From the second-floor window of the house the Company had loaned my brother Harry to use located by the main street of the town, you pretty much knew the owners of all of the vehicles since they were few and far between. A motorcycle with the "Kool Kat" on top of its front fender passed from time to time. Since the large Tela beach was not distant, and the sandy land contained the caves of numerous crabs, it wasn't at all unusual if a car ran over one of them.

I slept in the servant's room on the bottom floor. At night I could hear the old locomotive used to form trains moved back and forth pushing or pulling railroad cars like a restless ghost that could find no rest. I loved going to the Company Commissary and buying the thick slabs of bread pudding. I also liked purchasing military miniatures since despite my age of fourteen playing toy battles was a dear recreation to me.

Once in a while a black person would come to sell cassava bread. I really had only been close twice to a black person in Honduras. On Farm 19 we hired a black cook. She was excellent. I especially liked her waffles. But an American offered to pay her more and away she went. While at the Progreso American School as a boarding student a black lady would come to pick up my laundry. She was a sweet person and seemed to be no older than in her early forties. I was shocked when I heard that she had died. The cassava bread person came from Triunfo de la Cruz (Triumph of the Cross) seven kilometers from Tela. It is a settlement of Garifunas. These Afro-Honduran persons speak a mixture of Arawakan Indian language and other languages and some are mixture of African heritage plus native Indians. There are some English-speaking blacks who are considered Creoles. Blacks blend with the rest of the population and are admired for their music and success in sports. They have tended to live along the coast in Tela, La Ceiba,

Puerto Cortés, and the Bay Islands. On the Pacific Coast of Honduras are other blacks of mixed race called Miskitos.

Life among the population in Tela continued in its tranquil way. Americans mostly stayed in Tela Nueva since the Commissary would supply their needs. If something was not available the Commissary would order it for them. Teen Americans with more energy would wander into Tela Vieja crossing on foot the steel bridge of the Tela River that flowed nearby into the sea. My father made the remark that why would someone build a steel bridge so close to the ocean from which the salt air would rust it. Once in a great while I would take a dander to come to Tela Vieja the back way by crossing the river on the railroad trestle bridge. I had to be careful since missing the crossties would have me stepping into midair. I sure hoped that nothing would decide to come down the railroad track while I was doing the crossing. If you decided to go along the road of Tela Nueva towards its end you would come to the menial worker's barracks dwellings and continue on to the gravel paved airport. It was a great treat to me if I managed somehow to have someone pay my flight on a twin-engine propeller flown DC3 from Tela to Puerto Cortés to go see my mother in her two-story house that bordered the Puerto Cortes gravel-paved airport.

In Tela I was eating commissary food and drinking the slightly salty water. It was said that some sea water was added to extend the water supply. Everything seemed calm in Tela in 1954. And everything proceeded as usual. Just like Mount St. Helens in the United States, Tela was just another extinct volcano. It had seen troubled times when it struggled as a colony of Spain and during the Honduran revolutions but that was a while back. But changes were happening in Honduras that affected Tela. The old dictator Carías was getting on his seventies, and he allowed a fellow by the name of Gálvez to become president thinking that he would be his puppet. The new president passed reasonable laws that were what you would expect by the middle of the Twentieth Century such as an eight-hour work week and extra pay for working during holidays.

The Company was always interested in holding down costs. My father's small salary, which never was more than $165 a month was testimony to that. He really appreciated when my brother Georges would send him fifty dollars for a Christmas present. But you can't hold back the justifiable needs of the people forever. Sooner or later the cries for justice including economic justice reach a critical mass and then there's an explosion. So, it happened that while to my perception that every day in Tela was peaceful and routine, Company workers in Tela decided it was time to go on a wildcat strike concerning their pay. This happened in April of 1954. In May of the same year the men working the docks of Puerto Cortés felt that accordance with the law they should receive double their pay for working holidays.

The Company's reaction was to fire the dock worker's leader.

What it got in return was to have about all of its workers, about twenty-five thousand, to go on strike. They were joined by the workers of the Standard Fruit Company, the rival of United Fruit, numbering around fifteen thousand. Then the industrial workers of San Pedro Sula joined the strike. The strike went on for sixty-nine days, which was a miracle in itself for people with small resources and unsubstantial savings. But the merchants chipped in and gave out credit so that the strikers would be able to take care of their basic necessities. One result of the strike could be seen by noticing that the crabs that were plentiful around Tela disappeared.

One humorous situation was the intervention of the Honduran army. A contingent landed by plane and immediately placed a machine gun by the perimeter of the airfield. Their arrival went without incident. It seems that the soldiers paid attention to wild rumors that spoke of a dangerous armed insurrection by the workers. That is to say, a whole army of Communists equipped to the teeth with all sorts of weapons had taken oven the strike and were rampaging all over Tela. It all was so much hot air, and soon the soldiers were mingling with the population. In fact, they were riding about on jeeps showing off.

Another humorous incident took place closer to home. One day my brother Harry was riding on his Zundapp German motorcycle. As luck would have it, he approached a roadblock manned by strikers. Rather than listen to the demands of the strikers to turn back, he took out a pistol and aimed it at them and told them to let him through or else. The pistol was an ancient one. Since it didn't have a cylinder that flipped out, the bullets had to be loaded one by one into the rigid cylinder. The strikers let him through but from now on my brother in their minds was a scab, a strike breaker. While the strike was still on, Harry happened to be strolling in the park at Tela Vieja. He was recognized as having become an opponent to the strike. Some of the strikers tried to seize him, but he managed to escape but leaving his shirt behind since it was torn off in the struggle.

When the strike was over after sixty-nine days the worker's pay had a considerable increase, and they could lawfully form a syndicalist labor union.

As for my future, I no longer had a formal education to latch on. I was left to flop about like the proverbial fish out of the water. I thought that one possibility to pursue was to become an aircraft mechanic in the Honduran Air Force. At that time, it consisted of Corsair fighter bombers and DC3 transports obtained from the United States. With these hopes in mind, I obtained an application and recommendations from sympathetic people and headed to Tegucigalpa, the capital of Honduras I approached the guard and turned in my documents. I waited hoping that I would be accepted. I was disappointed. I was told that the man who had taken over the country as dictator, Julio Lozano Díaz, had run off to Miami after being deposed and had taken the country's treasury with him. Therefore, there would be no training funds available for the Air Force.

My father then thought that I could become a mechanic's apprentice in the shop owned by my brother Andrew's father, Raul Matute, in San Pedro Sula. I rode the family's bicycle back and forth from the shop hoping to gain automotive knowledge; but that was not to be. I received no instruction but only watched the mechanics at work. They made do with whatever tools could get to improvise and do their jobs replacing valves, changing cylinder rings, and so forth. I saw a mechanic trying to hold valves in place using a crowbar while he worked at them. This job approach so that I could gain an education didn't work out either.

While I was at his father's shop, my brother Andrew showed up. He had a good laugh when he got there. His Dad had taken a lathe and a piece of metal with the intention to turn it and carve a large screw with a ball attached at the end-a ball joint. What came out was a ball that looked like it was covered with fish scales. My brother attempted the same job and came out with a mechanical ball at the end of the screw that was smooth and lovely to admire.

My mother scraped the last money from her rent properties and was able to fund Andrew's emigration requirement that stated that an emigrant could enter the United states if he brought enough funds with him. This would indicate that he was a reliable person not intent on becoming another burden to America. Andrew worked a while in New Orleans as a toolmaker. Then he became a soldier in the US Army artillery. He was stationed on Okinawa. He told of there being on the island an atomic cannon, a huge artillery piece that was so long that it needed a prime mover at each end to haul it around. When it fired, it would shake up the whole island. After a while my brother ended in South Korea driving a deuce and a half Army water truck.

For my part, my family back in the States wanted to vouch for me. I was ready to emigrate also to the United States, and my brother Harry got me passage on a Company ship. But as I was looking forward to leave Honduras something absolutely ridiculous happened that stop my leaving. My mother had been leading a peaceful life in Puerto Cortés minding her own business. But she was vocal in supporting the Liberal Party. So, it came as surprise when she was arrested by supposedly taking part in a murder of a man in the company of a fellow murderer, two men that neither one of us had ever heard of at all. My mother remained in custody on the trumped-up charge. Since we had no money, we hired a lawyer who paid himself by going through my mother's remaining possessions and taking whatever he wanted to pay himself. This attorney never did do anything for my mother.

I was picked up for questioning. Of course, I didn't know anything about the whole stupid situation. Then we were transported in a Land Rover on our way to San Pedro Sula for further questioning. We were going on a road that was on the side of a cliff. I had to use all of my will power not to grab the steering wheel and plunge the car into the chasm. I might have killed the mean bastards transporting us, but then I had to think of my mother's safety. As it was, we arrived at the Little Fort, the same that had graced as a police station when we lived at barrio of El Benque during my childhood in better days. What an irony that was! The Little Fort when I was a kid seemed cute. But now I was on the receiving end of its evil purpose. I was confronted by an interrogator who placed electrodes taken from an old-style vertical telephone. He gave me a couple of small shocks by turning the telephone crank the so that I was aware that the setup worked and well. And it certainly hurt. Another irony. The type of telephone that we had enjoyed at the plantations now was being used as a torturing device.

What at one time brought pleasure now in the hands of an evil person would bring pain.

However, Divine Providence was on my side. I had shortly returned from Tegucigalpa and had stayed in the home of a cousin, José Cerón H. (The H stands for son in Spanish just like Jr. in English.). My cousin happened to be the personal secretary of the former dictator, Carías. When my police interrogator found out that I was connected to a powerful political figure, the interrogation ceased.

In fact, I went to stay with the sister of my cousin and her family at a place just outside of Puerto Cortés called Riomar meaning "Riversea" since there a river ran into the sea. My cousin Vicenta called "Chentilla" was a schoolteacher in Puerto Cortés. Her family added to the household funds by baking sweet rolls in an outdoor clay oven.

I had no further trouble with the police since it was obvious that for one thing I was out of town when the famous murder took place. But while the news of the murder and the capture of my mother and I being taken into questioning were causing an uproar, the yellow press had a field day. It was said that I was questioned and even hung up by the sack of my private part.

After I was released my mother remained in the prison of Puerto Cortés. She irritated her jailors by singing political songs of the Liberal Party. Her captors responded by locking her in a tower where she couldn't stretch out. But she kept on singing. They even took a hose and sprayed her with water while she was still inside the tower. My grandmother, another woman made of steel, would have been proud of her daughter. My mother stayed a prisoner and was transferred to a penitentiary in San Pedro Sula. No one had brought out any proof that she had been involved in the murder. But according to how the laws worked in Honduras, you were guilty until you could prove you were innocent. Due process as the rule of the land in the United States was inexistent in Honduras.

Chapter Twenty-two
A New Orientation

Once it was clear that I no longer would be pestered with stupid questions regarding the fictional criminals who conducted the murder, I had to decide what to do with my mother's property. The fact that we received financial military allowances from my brother helped a lot.

There were some really cheap apartments near to the home of my Aunt Vida in Puerto Cortés. So, I paid to have hauled all of my mother's things and stacked them literally to the ceiling for storage in one of the apartments on the second floor. It was one heck of a place. Once again, there appeared the unusual way of constructing the interior of a building. The interior walls of the cheap apartment did not reach all the way to the ceiling but instead left off about a foot from touching it. I had noticed this type of construction when it came to showers. Anyhow, in this apartment the top surface of the truncated wall was a highway—for rats! You could observe them coming and going every once in a while. My next-door neighbor stayed up on night and kept setting traps and killed dozens of them. I, for my part, set out a plantain loaded with rat poison. I had barely laid it on the floor of the apartment behind a stack of chairs than I felt that I need to check. Although it seemed such a short time after only five minutes, all I found was a smudge on the floor.

The windows of the apartment had no glass, not even screens. Their closure was made of planks nailed together. I soon found out that I had to be careful with liquids. Anything falling on the floor of my apartment rained on the apartment below. Since one of the women living below did had laundering for others to make some extra cash, she wouldn't appreciate getting my liquids on her freshly done ironed and starched items.

I now had to depend on my Aunt Vida to feed me allow me to use the bathroom since the toilet facilities of the apartment were beyond imagining. I had been acquainted with my aunt, Vida, and her husband, Luis, when my mother's and I would come to visit them right along with his daughters, Teodora, Norma, and Olga as well as Uncle Luis' daughter, Zoila, and her natural daughter, Myrna. It was indeed rare if they in turn came to visit us at a plantation. There was one visit that ended in a complete fiasco. My mother came to pick me up at El Progreso while I still attended the Progreso American School. Then we boarded a train on our way to Puerto Cortés. But at La Junta, a train junction, there was a misunderstanding as to which train wouldn't carry us to our final destination.

We found that we had boarded the wrong train. In the confusion, and as the wrong train started to move with us on board, my mother grabbed her suitcases and a bag of oranges destined for my aunt. My suitcase was left behind. In it were the Christmas presents I had received at the boarding school.

They weren't great treasures in the monetary sense, but for a kid with few toys, I really had looked forward to enjoying my Christmas gifts. When we arrived at Puerto Cortés my mother told my aunt of the sacrifice to bring her the oranges. But my aunt instead of being thankful made chide remarks that the oranges were no great deal. My aunt was always full of criticisms of my mother. Although she often may have been right about them, especially my mother's poor business sense, to my way of thinking—and I stayed quiet as a fellow not given to challenging older people-- there was no need that she as a grown woman should continue on and on with the sibling rivalry. After all they were women in their fifties and there was no need to maintain grudges from long ago. I liked my aunt, but her criticisms were not welcome, such as my mother's losing money by her trying to raise money with a truck and then a car used as a taxi as she strived to support us children while we went to school in San Pedro Sula.

My mother and I liked coming to Puerto Cortés even before she came to live there.

One of the attractions of Puerto Cortés were the Venetian Nights. What they consisted of having water craft appear at night on the secluded bay of the port with their lights aglow and fire off rockets and flares. One of the boats belonged to the Company. It was a remodeled PT boat left over as US Navy surplus from World War Two. The company used it for rapid transport of passengers between ports of Central America where it had installations. It also served as a vessel for pleasure cruises and fishing expeditions. Its name was Chamelecón being named after the Honduran river.

I went back and forth from Puerto Cortés to visit my mother in jail and then returned to be with my brother, Harry, in Tela. I stayed with him until he separated from his wife and left for other quarters. From there on I would have my father come visit me in Puerto Cortés from his place in San Pedro Sula. Or I would go see him.

While living in Puerto Cortés I sure was thankful for my aunt and her husband for looking after me. Uncle Luis had worked for the Company in its telegraph office in Puerto Cortés. His memory had been such that while young he could preserve, during a rush of customers wanting to send telegrams, as many as three messages in his brain until he got to transmitting them. Then later he became a train dispatcher for the Company. This turned out to be his downfall. The stress of keeping the various trains and rail motorcars from crashing into each other led to him having a nervous breakdown. By then he was an old man. He was about the same age of my father since both were born towards the end of the Nineteenth Century. He could not find work. He depended on my aunt to have boarders in their home and money from the rental house next door to their home and quarters near to the side of the house where he kept his tools.

I tried to help them any way I could since they were feeding me and looking after me.

For example, I would walk to the Company section of Puerto Cortés, go to the commissary, and bring back cans full of kerosene for my aunt's stove. Or I would help my uncle when he would have a building project by sitting on a plank and holding it stationary while he sawed.

My uncle had lived in New Orleans when young, and he had enjoyed the attractions of the pleasure area located at Spanish Fort that now has long disappeared. And he also lived in New York City. He had enjoyed roller skating down the streets with his companions. He also attended the operas of the Metropolitan Opera and would speak to me about the operas such as Norma and Figaro's Wedding. We would walk at night and go sit in the Puerto Cortés park just a couple of blocks from his home. I also would communicate to him what I had been learning through my correspondence courses. I also liked to accompany him as he walked to his Masonic lodge or go with him to the barber shop. I was like the son that he never had with my aunt.

At the time Puerto Cortés had as its core its waterfront businesses with wooden houses reminiscent of the ones you see in Western movies with wooden walkways in front of them and overhanging verandas. All that would eventually be destroyed after I left to emigrate to the United States to make room for greatly enlarged and modernized port facilities since Puerto Cortés has become the main port of Central America. Tela, that had been the location for the Company's headquarters in Honduras, gave way to the transfer of operations to La Lima.

The buildings of Tela belonging to the Company that I also cherished, the hospital where I was born, the great club facilities facing the wonderful Tela beach, and so forth became old and not suitable to modern times have been torn down. The concrete accounting building where my brother Harry worked for the Tela Railroad Company became an abandoned shell. The sea-going pier that made Tela a port burned down and was not replaced. The Company's empire disappeared. It lost interest in running the banana the day-to-day operations of the banana business. Independent contractors became responsible for the banana production. The Company, with its control now freed, became interested in the distribution and sale of the bananas exclusively. It now no longer needed to operate railroads and the facilities that took care of its workers such as its hospitals. Its sprawling empire of personal facilities ceased to exist.

Gone were the colorful days when banana stems were transported by first by mules and then loaded to railcars and sent to the ports of Tela or Puerto Cortés. Gone also was the unloading of the banana stems at the ports by means of conveyor belts sent into the holds of refrigerator ships called, "reefers." This kind of processing was highlighted in the song "Day-O (The Banana Song). It mentions loading the banana stems "till the morning comes." This is correct when dealing with bananas. The temperature when they are found at their best is the coolest parts of the day including harvesting in the early morning. Nowadays the stems are placed on trailers to be transported to sheds were the stems are taken apart and the banana bunches are packed into cardboard boxes and placed in shipping containers, loaded onto trucks that transport them to Puerto Cortés, and then placed into container ships. Thus, there was no longer any use for mules, cargo trains, and the conveyor belts of the Tela wharf meant it that was becoming obsolete even before it burned.

With the accounting department of the Company in Tela, my brother Harry needed to secure new employment. He found it with the Rosario Mining Company at El Mochito. This location proved to be a wealthy investment since it produced a lot of silver.

My visits made my mother's stay at the penitentiary more satisfying. But there is no substitute for freedom, and she was finally let out after the whole farce had died down after having served almost two years for nothing.

I also felt so bad for a rich Jewish merchant who was obviously being bled white financially by lawyers as he was also being charged with trumped-up charges.

My brother, Andrew, was by now honorably discharged from the US Army and was sponsoring me to come to America. I went to the US consulate in San Pedro Sula and presented my papers and was accepted to become an American resident. I loved to see Old Glory fluttering over the facility. Through my life in the Company and my attendance at the American Schools I could say that I was truly prepared to live in the United States. It only remained for me to find a way to travel. My father suggested that I write a letter to the Company asking them to please help me out. The Company came through to my everlasting gratitude.

I sailed away in early 1958 on the good ship MV Leon from Puerto Cortés. The vessel then went to Puerto Barrios, Guatemala. There it did not find enough coffee cargo, and we returned to Puerto Cortés. I got off the ship and lo and behold I ran into my mother at one of the seaport waterfront stores. Was she ever surprised to see me again! I finally arrived at Galveston, Texas, where my brother Andy was staying.

I had but twenty dollars in my wallet.

Here you see the Zwez family in Switzerland in the late 1940s. The taller girl at the left is my niece Stephanie, called "Steffi," with her mother next to her, Marie-Louise, and then the smaller girl, my niece Annelise, and on the extreme right checking his watch is my brother Georges, called "George."

The family lived at Neuhausem am Rheinfall right next to the famous Swiss Rhine Falls.

My brother also stayed at a vacation home on Lake Bienne. The house had belonged to his wife's father, a Calvinist pastor. One of the floors of this once-Catholic convent housed a vast collection of arrowheads that came from the bottom of the lake as they appeared on shore when stirred up by storms. They were made by the famous Swiss lake dwellers of prehistoric times.

George had come over from Switzerland with my father to Mercedes, Texas. And he continued on with Dad when they emigrated to Honduras, and he also worked for the United Fruit Company. My brother returned to Switzerland. I did not get to meet him until he came to New Orleans in 1962. He was outstanding in that he kept up his correspondence with us.

He was generous with our father and even sent him a Bulova watch. For Christmas and for my father's birthday, he would send a fifty-dollar check. Since my father never made more than one hundred sixty-five dollars a month because he had lived on the plantations where practically everything was provided for him, the extra dollars were very welcome.

This photograph shows how prosperous my Swiss brother had become. He had done well to leave a steady, but not so very promising livelihood as far as rising opportunities. George was an inspiration to all of us in Honduras as someone who had left and really had done well for himself.

Here is Aunt Vida. My Uncle Luis Murillo was uncle by marriage to my aunt. They were living in Puerto Cortes, the main banana port of Honduras, a wonderful deep-water port, and indeed the main one of Central America.

While the port location is excellent for the docking—ocean-going ships can drop anchor right at the shoreline. Inland the situation was a lot less favorable. The area was swampy and there were lots that were submerged. In order to build you had to fill your lot with sand. That was no end in sight since the sand would tend to settle and if a lot next door was watery you had to haul in more sand to keep your lot from liquifying.

My Uncle Luis had been a train dispatcher for United Fruit. He had to quit when he had a nervous breakdown. My Aunt Vida kept the family going by taking in boarders.

My aunt and uncle were of those beautiful people that appear in your life and now are gone. They kept me going for about two years both materially and spiritually while my poor, innocent mother was kept in prison. I and my uncle got really close, and he was like a second father to me.

In February of 1958 I emigrated to the United States. I had always admired the military so as soon as would enter my new home country, I was looking forward to enlisting.

I preferred joining the Army since it has only a three-year enlistment as opposed to the Navy and the Air Force that demanded a four-year hitch. I wanted to have my service to my new country to be a token of gratitude as well as a start in my life that would allow me to get my feet firmly on the ground.

When I told the American consul in San Pedro Sula that I wanted to enlist in the Army as soon as I arrived in America, he said, keeping in mind that in those days many were unwillingly drafted, "People hate being in the Army."

Obviously, his discouraging words did not deter me. But as this photograph too graphically reveals, while I was looking forward to my life in the States, I was a little nervous and uncertain as to what was awaiting me in my new situations.

As much as enjoyed life aboard the United Fruit Company ships and having been born and spent life at ports, later on I did join the Naval Reserve.

The United Fruit Company did me a last favor by giving me free passage to America on one of its ships that was comfortable and luxurious.